Learning Bulma

Understand How to Develop Responsive, Mobile-first Websites Using This Impressive, Modern Framework

Aravind Shenoy

Apress®

Learning Bulma

Aravind Shenoy
Mumbai, Maharashtra, India

ISBN-13 (pbk): 978-1-4842-5481-3   ISBN-13 (electronic): 978-1-4842-5482-0
https://doi.org/10.1007/978-1-4842-5482-0

Managing Director, Apress Media LLC: Welmoed Spahr
Acquisitions Editor: Louise Corrigan
Development Editor: James Markham
Coordinating Editor: Nancy Chen

Cover designed by eStudioCalamar

Cover image designed by Freepik (www.freepik.com)

Distributed to the book trade worldwide by Springer Science+Business Media New York, 233 Spring Street, 6th Floor, New York, NY 10013. Phone 1-800-SPRINGER, fax (201) 348-4505, e-mail orders-ny@springer-sbm.com, or visit www.springeronline.com. Apress Media, LLC is a California LLC and the sole member (owner) is Springer Science + Business Media Finance Inc (SSBM Finance Inc). SSBM Finance Inc is a **Delaware** corporation.

For information on translations, please e-mail rights@apress.com, or visit www.apress.com/rights-permissions.

Apress titles may be purchased in bulk for academic, corporate, or promotional use. eBook versions and licenses are also available for most titles. For more information, reference our Print and eBook Bulk Sales web page at www.apress.com/bulk-sales.

Any source code or other supplementary material referenced by the author in this book is available to readers on GitHub via the book's product page, located at www.apress.com/9781484254813. For more detailed information, please visit http://www.apress.com/source-code.

Printed on acid-free paper

*I dedicate this book to my mother **Vatsala Shenoy**;
she indeed is my rock. She stood by me all my life
without any expectations and completely accepted me
the way I am (despite me being a misfit☺). Without her,
I would have never written a book in the first place.
The immense support and unconditional love from my
mother is very much a part of my success. I don't want to
say anything more, as it will spoil what I want to convey*

Table of Contents

About the Author

Aravind Shenoy is a Senior Technical/Content writer by profession, whose core interests are technical writing, content writing, information development, web design, and business analysis. He was born and raised in Mumbai. A music buff , he loves listening to rock n' roll & rap. Oasis, R.E.M, The Doors, Dire Straits, Coldplay, 3 Doors Down, Jimi Hendrix, Cranberries, U2, Prodigy, and Michael Jackson rule his playlists.

An engineering graduate from the Manipal Institute of Technology and author of several books, he is a keen learner and believes there is always a steep learning curve in this walk of life. In summary, he quips: "The most important thing is to be happy. After all, we're here for a good time, not a long time. Maybe... Definitely maybe." ☺

About the Technical Reviewer

 **Alexander Chinedu Nnakwue** has a background in Mechanical Engineering from the University of Ibadan, Nigeria and has been a front-end developer for more than 3 years, working on both web and mobile technologies. He also has experience as a technical author, writer, and reviewer. He enjoys programming for the Web, and occasionally you can also find him playing soccer. He was born in Benin City and is currently based in Lagos, Nigeria.

Acknowledgments

This is the 5th book I've written for Apress and 11th overall. I would like to thank Apress and its editorial team including Nancy, Louise, and Jim for collaborating and effectively helping me. I would also like to thank my reviewer, Alexander Chinedu Nnakwue, who provided me great insights while writing this book. I wish all of you well in this walk of life.

CHAPTER 1

Jumpstart Bulma

Bulma (`https://bulma.io/`) is an open source web design framework that is used to create immersive web sites. Bulma is a powerful CSS framework for designing scalable front-end code quickly and effectively. Adhering to a mobile-first paradigm, it comes with built-in CSS components for creating responsive web sites. The beauty of Bulma is that it abstracts the pain of scratch-coding by providing you with the tools and utilities to create interactive web sites in a hassle-free, time-saving way.

Prior to moving ahead, we need to understand the usability of CSS frameworks in web design. Aspects like cross-browser computability, consistency, and the speed of developing web apps/sites add to the arduous task of constructing an efficient layout and a feature-rich web site. Beginners need to remember that all CSS frameworks come with predesigned sets of reusable code and modules that not only speed up development time but also take the guesswork out of complex styling. This also results in clean coding and ensures that your web sites scale properly over devices of any make or screen/device size.

This book is aimed at introducing you to the basic properties of Bulma in an easy-to-comprehend manner. Bulma's baked-in new grid system, layout, content modules, typography, helper classes, media, and forms help design robust user interfaces without the bulk or clutter associated with heavyweight frameworks. Moreover, adhering to a mobile-first philosophy, it eliminates the pain and bottlenecks of developing intuitive web sites for smartphones, tablets, and compact platforms.

© Aravind Shenoy 2020
A. Shenoy, *Learning Bulma*, https://doi.org/10.1007/978-1-4842-5482-0_1

In the next section, we will explore the differences between mobile-first and responsive design that will help budding web designers understand the basic concepts coherently.

Mobile-First vs. Responsive Web Design

Mobile-first design involves building a web site/app for the mobile platform. Once the site has been designed, it is tweaked for the bigger screens/bigger devices like tablets, desktops, or large display screens. It is all about creating an immersive user experience on smartphones and other small-screen mobile devices (akin to the progressive enhancement ideology). If the majority of your users are mobile users, then this approach will be optimal. It is tailored to fill all the gaps specifically for mobile devices, but may lack in certain aspects when it comes to traditional desktop site versions.

In contrast, responsive web design is inclined toward traditional desktops and then tweaked for smaller screens/devices. It is tailored for creating an immersive user experience on normal-sized desktops and large display screens (akin to the graceful degradation ideology). If your target audience is desktop users, then this approach will be optimal; however, it lacks certain aspects when it comes to mobile phones or small screen compact devices.

Mobile App/Sites—the De facto Standard for Google

Starting July 2019, according to reports (`https://developers.google.com/search/mobile-sites/mobile-first-indexing`), Google has focused on the default indexing of mobile sites rather than the traditional desktop web site version. Google stated that mobile-first indexing is the preferable method, as most users tend to view and publish information on mobile-platforms.

Google has stressed the fact that the information on the mobile and desktop versions of the web sites should be the same, inclusive of the titles, structured data, and metadescription. Older web sites will be indexed until the mobile web pages are designed.

Studies (`www.statista.com/topics/779/mobile-internet/`) have suggested that mobile data traffic is going to grow manifold, at least seven-fold by 2022. With four billion unique mobile users by April 2019, and 48% of web pages worldwide accessed through the smartphone platform, mobile-first is the way to go.

Both mobile-first and responsive web design preference depend on the current technological advances and target audience. For example, a recent study (`https://darwindigital.com/mobile-first-versus-responsive-web-design/`) concluded that B2B companies still showed interest in responsive design, with most users checking out the products/services/solutions on the desktop web site version.

Now, let's get started with Bulma and become acquainted with the inner workings of this easy-to-understand web design framework in the next section.

Jump-Start Bulma

Bulma, being mobile-first, is tailor-made for mobile devices, but with a few tweaks it can be optimized for traditional desktops too. Keep in mind that it was created keeping mobile platforms as the crux, therefore the web sites you design using Bulma are in line with Google's current and future trends. It definitely is SEO-friendly and future-proof as Google leans toward mobile web sites for indexing purposes compared to conventional desktop versions.

To access the Bulma official web site, use the following:

```
https://bulma.io
```

The mobile site version of the Bulma official web page is shown in Figure 1-1.

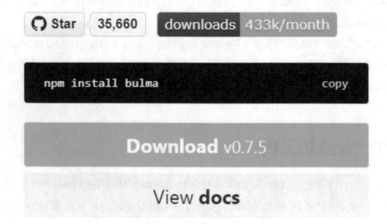

Figure 1-1. *Bulma mobile site*

The desktop site version of the Bulma official web page is shown in Figure 1-2.

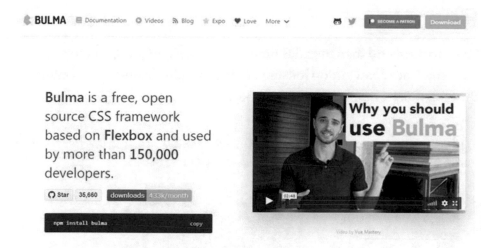

Figure 1-2. *Bulma desktop site*

From the preceding screenshots, you can see that the content of the desktop site and mobile site are the same but are displayed differently owing to the larger desktop and smaller mobile screens.

However, remember that Bulma is mobile-first in nature, meaning it is tailored for mobile platforms and can then be optimized for tablets and large desktops with minimum tweaks.

Now that we have a brief idea about the responsiveness of this mobile-inclined framework, we will move forward to the installation process in the next section.

Installing Bulma

There are three specific ways of installing Bulma, and you can choose any one of them as per your business and design requirements.

Method I

To download and then install Bulma for your web projects, you need to click the Download button located at the top-right section of the Bulma desktop official home page (Figure 1-3).

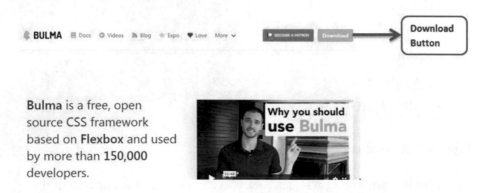

Figure 1-3. Download button for installing Bulma zip file

On downloading, you will get the Bulma zip file. On unzipping the Bulma zip file, you can see the different files and folders, which have the file structure shown in Figure 1-4.

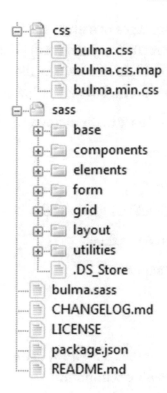

Figure 1-4. *File structure of the downloaded and unzipped Bulma framework (latest version 0.7.5)*

You can include the link to this file in your HTML page to use it at the basic level.

Method II

Another way to include Bulma is by using the CDN link for the Bulma framework:

```
<link rel="stylesheet" href="https://cdnjs.cloudflare.com/ajax/
libs/bulma/0.7.5/css/bulma.min.css">
```

There are several advantages of using a CDN file for your web projects. For starters, a CDN (content delivery network) holds copies of your file in several locations across multiple servers. The files can be images, fonts, scripts, or videos. The benefits include the following:

- More servers and easy maintenance

- More bandwidth

- High performance

- Redundancy for fail-safe protection

- Optimized caching settings

- Parallelized downloads

Method III

You can use Node Package Manager (NPM) to install the Bulma package, specifically using the following command:

```
npm install bulma
```

The entire process of installing Node.js on Windows is explained in the following link:

https://blog.teamtreehouse.com/install-node-js-npm-windows.

For Android and Linux distributions, you can take a look at the following link:

https://nodejs.org/en/download/package-manager/.

Note*- Icons in Bulma can be included by using the Font Awesome 5 link:

```
<script defer src="https://use.fontawesome.com/releases/v5.3.1/js/all.js"></script>
```

Summary

In this chapter, we saw an overview of the easy-to-use Bulma framework. We looked at the differences between mobile-first and responsive web design, and how things are going to shape up in the present and the near future. Moving forward, we looked at the different methods of installing Bulma in your web projects. The next chapter will explain the grid system and utility classes that will enable you to get to grips with this powerful web design toolkit.

CHAPTER 2

Grids and Utility Classes

Bulma is an intuitive framework adhering to the mobile-first approach. In this well-connected era, people prefer mobile web sites compared with traditional desktop web sites and other media. Moreover, a mobile-first paradigm accounts for better semantics, simplified code structure, and a superlative user experience.

Bulma is genetically tailored for the mobile platform. It includes simple modules and components; using them, your web site can be tweaked for desktop and widescreen display too. Bulma follows a minimalistic approach, as the focus is completely on interactive web site design and rapid development

In this chapter, we will learn about grids and utility classes in Bulma including columns, offsets, gaps, and helper classes that render ultimate flexibility and simplicity for creating immersive web sites.

Note: In this book, we will be using Notepad++ as the default editor for all the code examples. Sample content from `www.catipsum.com` is used for the code examples in the book.

The best way to learn web design is to start coding and learning it practically instead of wandering through loads of theory—so let's start working with Bulma immediately.

© Aravind Shenoy 2020
A. Shenoy, *Learning Bulma*, https://doi.org/10.1007/978-1-4842-5482-0_2

Bulma Prototype/Starter Template

Like all CSS frameworks, Bulma has the basic prototype with the CDN and supported icon links that will be a part of all the code examples in this book.

Listing 2-1 depicts the Bulma starter template with all the necessary links and attributes.

Listing 2-1. Bulma Starter Template

```
<!DOCTYPE html>
<html>
  <head>
    <meta charset="utf-8">
    <meta name="viewport" content="width=device-width, initial-
    scale=1">
    <title>Hello Bulma!</title>
    <link rel="stylesheet" href="https://cdnjs.cloudflare.com/
    ajax/libs/bulma/0.7.5/css/bulma.min.css">
    <script defer src="https://use.fontawesome.com/releases/
    v5.3.1/js/all.js"></script>
  </head>
  <body>
  <section class="section">
    <div class="container">
      <h1 class="title">
        Welcome to Bulma- a simple and effective framework
      </h1>
    </div>
  </section>
  </body>
</html>
```

In Listing 2-1, you can see the various links and styles in the *<head>* section. In the *<head>* section, the charset *meta* tag is used to define an HTML document's character set. The viewport *meta* tag helps web designers control the *viewport* (viewport is the portion of the web page visible to the users). While the *width=device-width* attribute sets the width of the page as per the device screen, *initial-scale=1.0* instructs the device to display the page without any zooming.

Next, we define the following CDN link for incorporating Bulma's ingrained CSS styles:

```
<link rel="stylesheet" href="https://cdnjs.cloudflare.com/ajax/
libs/bulma/0.7.5/css/bulma.min.css">
```

In addition, you can use the Font Awesome icons by using the following JavaScript link:

```
<script defer src="https://use.fontawesome.com/releases/v5.3.1/
js/all.js"></script>
```

Finally, after placing all the required links in the <head> tag, we proceed with the <body> tags where we write the code and markup for the output. This basic starter template will be used for all the examples in the book. In the next section, we will learn about the Flexbox-powered grid layouts.

Flexbox-Powered Grid Layout

A grid layout helps achieve good readability, higher flexibility, and page cohesiveness. Bulma is a mobile-first framework, where you create a mobile web site and then tweak it for the desktop interface.

The 12-column grid layout in Bulma is easy to understand. By default, all the columns in Bulma will be stacked on top of each other, owing to its mobile-first paradigm. Thereon, by adding different classes and attributes, columns are defined in a default 12-column grid structure.

In Bulma, columns are defined as per their size and varying classes to create the grid. Bulma's Flexbox-powered grid depicts excellent adaptability with the mobile platform. Even customizing it for tablet, desktop, and widescreen size-screens is quite simple; Bulma is purely CSS-based and, with minimal use of JavaScript, you can build responsive, interactive sites quickly and easily.

Well-equipped with a plethora of alternative styles, all you need to do is use **is—** or **has—** as the modifiers. Bulma columns are defined with a columns container with a *<div>* element using the ***columns*** class. Then, within this main columns container, you need to define columns with the ***column*** class. Listing 2-2 shows the prototype for constructing columns. It contains a columns container and four columns.

Listing 2-2. Basic Column Structure

```
<div class="columns">
  <div class="column">
    First column
  </div>
  <div class="column">
    Second column
  </div>
  <div class="column">
    Third column
  </div>
  <div class="column">
    Fourth column
  </div>
</div>
```

Listing 2-3 shows an example of how columns are displayed on a mobile and desktop screen.

Listing 2-3. Grid-Based Columns

```
<body>
  <div class="columns">
            <div class="column" style="background-color: #7CFC00;">
            cat ipsum dolor sit amet, eos, nostrum and
            aspernatur. Eum. Nisi corporis so velit. Rem vitae.
            Do irure. Sed. Corporis ab or in perspiciatis.cat
            ipsum dolor sit amet, eos, nostrum and aspernatur.
            Eum. Nisi corporis so velit. Rem vitae. Do irure.
            Sed. Corporis ab or in perspiciatis.
            </div>

            <div class="column" style="background-color: #FFFF00;">
            cat ipsum dolor sit amet, eos, nostrum and
            aspernatur. Eum. Nisi corporis so velit. Rem vitae.
            Do irure. Sed. Corporis ab or in perspiciatis.cat
            ipsum dolor sit amet, eos, nostrum and aspernatur.
            Eum. Nisi corporis so velit. Rem vitae. Do irure.
            Sed. Corporis ab or in perspiciatis.
            </div>

            <div class="column" style="background-color: #E0FFFF;">
            cat ipsum dolor sit amet, eos, nostrum and
            aspernatur. Eum. Nisi corporis so velit. Rem vitae.
            Do irure. Sed. Corporis ab or in perspiciatis.cat
            ipsum dolor sit amet, eos, nostrum and aspernatur.
            Eum. Nisi corporis so velit. Rem vitae. Do irure.
            Sed. Corporis ab or in perspiciatis.
            </div>
```

```
<div class="column" style="background-color: #FFEBCD;">
cat ipsum dolor sit amet, eos, nostrum and
aspernatur. Eum. Nisi corporis so velit. Rem vitae.
Do irure. Sed. Corporis ab or in perspiciatis.cat
ipsum dolor sit amet, eos, nostrum and aspernatur.
Eum. Nisi corporis so velit. Rem vitae. Do irure.
Sed. Corporis ab or in perspiciatis.
</div>
</div>
</body>
```

As seen in the preceding code, we define a container with the **columns** class. Inside it, we define four columns using the **column** class. Each column has the **cat ipsum** sample text. (*In further code examples, the entire sample content from cat ipsum will not be shown; it will just be denoted by "cat ipsum dolor sit eos..."*)

With each column, we also define the **background color** using the inline style CSS code.

The output of this code on a small screen or mobile phone is shown in Figure 2-1.

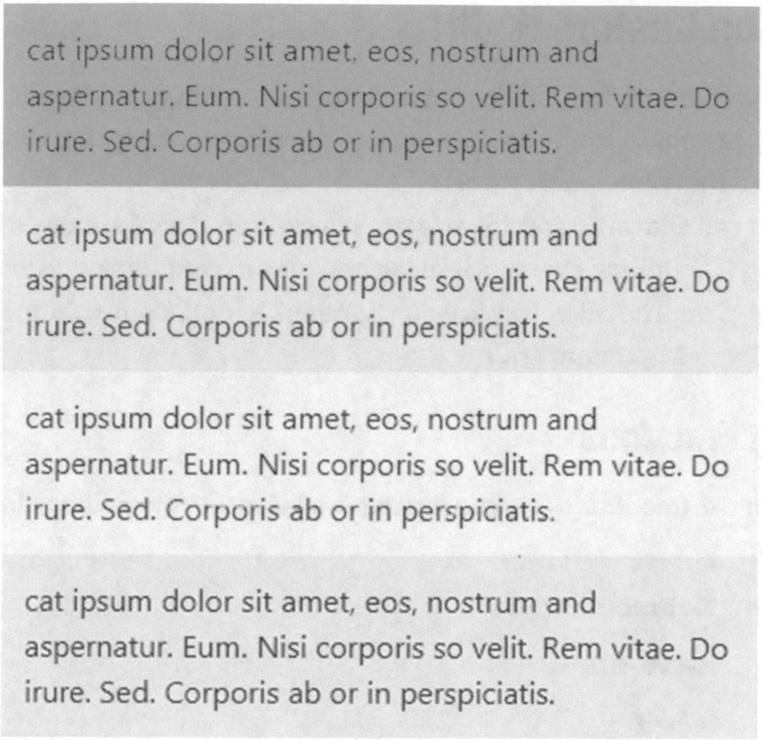

cat ipsum dolor sit amet, eos, nostrum and aspernatur. Eum. Nisi corporis so velit. Rem vitae. Do irure. Sed. Corporis ab or in perspiciatis.

cat ipsum dolor sit amet, eos, nostrum and aspernatur. Eum. Nisi corporis so velit. Rem vitae. Do irure. Sed. Corporis ab or in perspiciatis.

cat ipsum dolor sit amet, eos, nostrum and aspernatur. Eum. Nisi corporis so velit. Rem vitae. Do irure. Sed. Corporis ab or in perspiciatis.

cat ipsum dolor sit amet, eos, nostrum and aspernatur. Eum. Nisi corporis so velit. Rem vitae. Do irure. Sed. Corporis ab or in perspiciatis.

Figure 2-1. *Columns on a mobile site*

On a desktop screen, the columns are next to each other as shown in Figure 2-2.

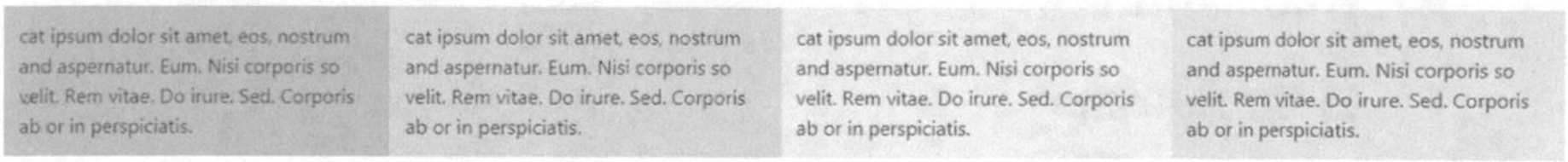

cat ipsum dolor sit amet, eos, nostrum and aspernatur. Eum. Nisi corporis so velit. Rem vitae. Do irure. Sed. Corporis ab or in perspiciatis. | cat ipsum dolor sit amet, eos, nostrum and aspernatur. Eum. Nisi corporis so velit. Rem vitae. Do irure. Sed. Corporis ab or in perspiciatis. | cat ipsum dolor sit amet, eos, nostrum and aspernatur. Eum. Nisi corporis so velit. Rem vitae. Do irure. Sed. Corporis ab or in perspiciatis. | cat ipsum dolor sit amet, eos, nostrum and aspernatur. Eum. Nisi corporis so velit. Rem vitae. Do irure. Sed. Corporis ab or in perspiciatis.

Figure 2-2. *Output on a desktop site*

As you can see, the columns are responsive because they adapt well to the desktop size screen as well. You will also observe that if the width is not specified, all the columns automatically have equal width.

Adding Custom Width

Although the columns have equal width in a 12-column grid layout, the settings are not in stone. You can change the width by assigning custom values to the column size.

You can allocate a specific size to each column. There are several ways of doing it in Bulma. One way is using fractions in conjunction with the column class. The other way is using numbers to define the column size for a default 12-column grid.

Using Fractions

You can use fractions to denote the required size. Let's look the following classes:

- **is-three-quarters**

- **is-two-thirds**

- **is-half**

- **is-one-third**

- **is-one-quarter**

- **is-full**

- **is-four-fifths**

- **is-three-fifths**

- **is-two-fifths**

- **is-one-fifth**

  The **is-three-quarters** class will span 3/4th space of the default 12-column grid.

The **is-one-quarter** class will span 1/4th space of the default 12-column grid.

The **is-full** class will span the full width of the default 12-column grid.

Remember that the other columns whose size is not defined will automatically fill up the remaining space. As you can see in Listing 2-4, once we define the columns container, we assign the **column is-one-fifth**, **column is-three-fifth**, and **column** classes to the three columns, respectively.

Listing 2-4. Defining Grid Column Size Using Fractions

```
<div class="columns">
    <div class="column is-one-fifth" style="border:5px solid
    Tomato;">
    cat ipsum dolor sit amet...
    </div>

    <div class="column is-three-fifth" style="border:5px solid
    DodgerBlue;">
    cat ipsum dolor sit amet...
    </div>

    <div class="column" style="border:5px solid Violet;">
    cat ipsum dolor sit amet...
    </div>

</div>
```

Though some of you are familiar with basic CSS and HTML, the following link is included for learning basic CSS easily:

www.quackit.com

The preceding link will get you acquainted with intermediate-grade CSS and is also a good reference.

The one-fifth size spans 1/5th length of a 12-column grid and the three-fifth size spans 3/5th length of a 12-column grid. Since the third column size is not specified, it will automatically occupy the remaining space. The output of the code on a mobile phone, and then on a traditional desktop interface, are shown in the following screenshots.

Colored borders were also assigned to all the columns. You will see that in Figure 2-3 the columns are, by default, stacked on top of each other for a mobile screen, whereas on the desktop interface in Figure 2-4 the columns depict the size as defined in the code.

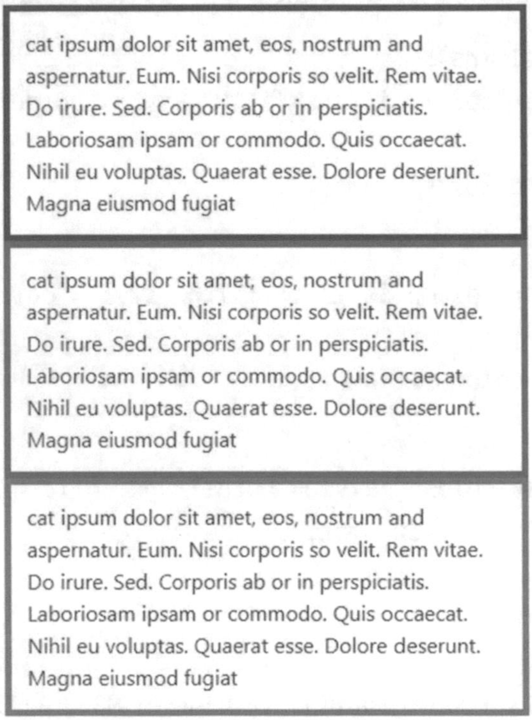

Figure 2-3. *Output on a mobile site*

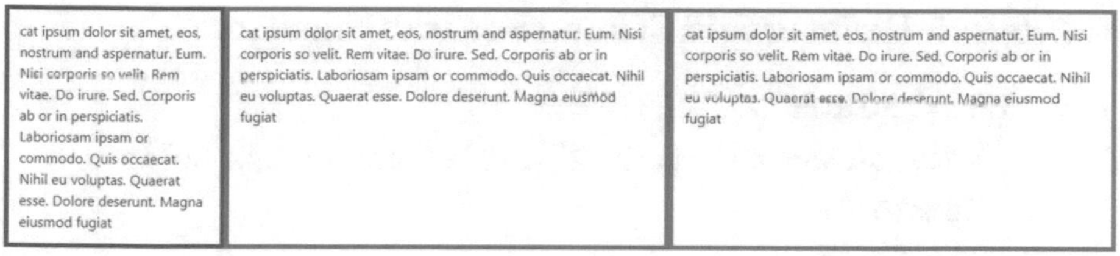

cat ipsum dolor sit amet, eos, nostrum and aspernatur. Eum. Nisi corporis so velit. Rem vitae. Do irure. Sed. Corporis ab or in perspiciatis. Laboriosam ipsam or commodo. Quis occaecat. Nihil eu voluptas. Quaerat esse. Dolore deserunt. Magna eiusmod fugiat

cat ipsum dolor sit amet, eos, nostrum and aspernatur. Eum. Nisi corporis so velit. Rem vitae. Do irure. Sed. Corporis ab or in perspiciatis. Laboriosam ipsam or commodo. Quis occaecat. Nihil eu voluptas. Quaerat esse. Dolore deserunt. Magna eiusmod fugiat

cat ipsum dolor sit amet, eos, nostrum and aspernatur. Eum. Nisi corporis so velit. Rem vitae. Do irure. Sed. Corporis ab or in perspiciatis. Laboriosam ipsam or commodo. Quis occaecat. Nihil eu voluptas. Quaerat esse. Dolore deserunt. Magna eiusmod fugiat

Figure 2-4. *Output on a desktop site*

Using Plain Numbers

Owing to a 12-column layout, the following syntax can also be used for defining the size of the columns:

- is-1

- is-2

- is-3

- is-4

- is-5

- is-6

- is-7

- is-8

- is-9

- is-10

- is-11

- is-12

The **is-1** class will span a length equivalent to 1 column in a default 12-column grid. Similarly, the **is-9** class will span the equivalent of 9 columns for a 12-column horizontal column grid (Listing 2-5).

Listing 2-5. Defining Grid Column Size with Numbers

```
<div class="columns">
        <div class="column is-2" style="border:5px solid
        Tomato;">
        cat ipsum dolor sit amet.....
        </div>

        <div class="column is-7" style="border:5px solid
        DodgerBlue;">
        cat ipsum dolor sit amet.....
        </div>

        <div class="column" style="border:5px solid Violet;">
        cat ipsum dolor sit amet.....
        </div>
</div>
```

As per the preceding code, the column element with the **is-2** class will occupy the space of 2 columns, whereas the column element with the **is-7** will occupy the space of 7 columns. The element with the **column** class, which has not been allocated a specific size, will occupy the remaining space.

The output of the code on the mobile and desktop interfaces is shown in Figure 2-5 and Figure 2-6 respectively.

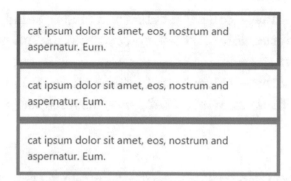

Figure 2-5. *Output on a mobile site*

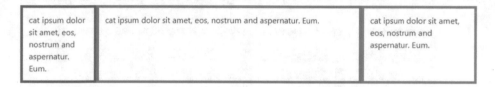

Figure 2-6. *Output on a desktop site*

Observe that the elements are stacked on top of each other by default. However, if you want the mobile version to show the same number of columns as the desktop interface, you can add the **is-mobile** class to the **columns** container class (Listing 2-6).

Listing 2-6. Implementing Desktop-Like Column Structure for Mobile Screens

```
<div class="columns is-mobile">
        <div class="column" style="border:5px solid Fuchsia;">
        cat ipsum dolor sit amet, eos, nostrum and aspernatur...
        </div>
        <div class="column" style="border:5px solid DarkCyan;">
        cat ipsum dolor sit amet, eos, nostrum and aspernatur...
        </div>
```

```
        <div class="column" style="border:5px solid Red;">
        cat ipsum dolor sit amet, eos, nostrum and aspernatu...
        </div>
        <div class="column" style="border:5px solid Lime;">
        cat ipsum dolor sit amet, eos, nostrum and aspernatur...
        <div>
</div>
```

The **is-mobile** class facilitates the display of four columns, akin to the desktop interface. The output of the code on a mobile platform and desktop platform, respectively are displayed in Figure 2-7 and Figure 2-8 respectively.

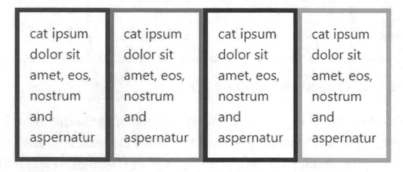

Figure 2-7. *Output on a mobile site*

cat ipsum dolor sit amet, eos, nostrum and aspernatur	cat ipsum dolor sit amet, eos, nostrum and aspernatur	cat ipsum dolor sit amet, eos, nostrum and aspernatur	cat ipsum dolor sit amet, eos, nostrum and aspernatur

Figure 2-8. *Output on a desktop site*

Multiline Columns

In Bulma, by default, the number of columns defined within the columns container are placed in a single row. If you want to define the next row, you usually use another columns container and define columns for that container.

However, you can use more rows using a single columns container by adding an **is-multiline** class (Listing 2-7). That way, all the included columns within that container will occupy space as per the defined size. Once the space of a 12-column grid is occupied, the following columns will occupy the defined space in the next row.

Listing 2-7. Multiline Columns Component

```
<div class="columns is-multiline">

        <div class="column is-2" style="background-color:
        #7CFC00;">
        cat ipsum dolor cat ipsum dolor sit amet, eos..
        </div>

        <div class="column is-10" style="background-color:
        #FFFF00;">
        cat ipsum dolor cat ipsum dolor sit amet, eos...
        </div>

        <div class="column is-9" style="background-color:
        #E0FFFF">
        cat ipsum dolor cat ipsum dolor sit amet, eos...
        </div>

        <div class="column is-3" style="background-color:
        #FFEBCD">
        cat ipsum dolor cat ipsum dolor sit amet, eos...
        </div>
</div>
```

In Figure 2-9, the columns occupy the defined width and shift to the second row after the 12-column width is surpassed.

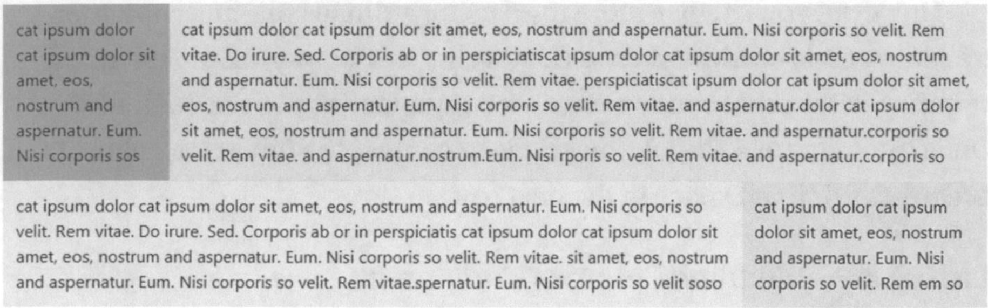
cat ipsum dolor cat ipsum dolor sit amet, eos, nostrum and aspernatur. Eum. Nisi corporis sos
cat ipsum dolor cat ipsum dolor sit amet, eos, nostrum and aspernatur. Eum. Nisi corporis so velit. Rem vitae. Do irure. Sed. Corporis ab or in perspiciatiscat ipsum dolor cat ipsum dolor sit amet, eos, nostrum and aspernatur. Eum. Nisi corporis so velit. Rem vitae. perspiciatiscat ipsum dolor cat ipsum dolor sit amet, eos, nostrum and aspernatur. Eum. Nisi corporis so velit. Rem vitae. and aspernatur.dolor cat ipsum dolor sit amet, eos, nostrum and aspernatur. Eum. Nisi corporis so velit. Rem vitae. and aspernatur.corporis so velit. Rem vitae. and aspernatur.nostrum.Eum. Nisi rporis so velit. Rem vitae. and aspernatur.corporis so
cat ipsum dolor cat ipsum dolor sit amet, eos, nostrum and aspernatur. Eum. Nisi corporis so velit. Rem vitae. Do irure. Sed. Corporis ab or in perspiciatis cat ipsum dolor cat ipsum dolor sit amet, eos, nostrum and aspernatur. Eum. Nisi corporis so velit. Rem vitae. sit amet, eos, nostrum and aspernatur. Eum. Nisi corporis so velit. Rem vitae.spernatur. Eum. Nisi corporis so velit soso
cat ipsum dolor cat ipsum dolor sit amet, eos, nostrum and aspernatur. Eum. Nisi corporis so velit. Rem em so

Figure 2-9. *Multiline columns*

The **column is-2** and **column is-10** classes for the first two elements enable it to occupy the first row. In the next row, you can see the remaining two elements with the **column is-9** and **column is-3** class.

Gaps

In Bulma, the default gap size on each side of a column is equal to **0.75rem**. That effectively increases to **1.5rem** between the two adjacent columns. Looking at the previous multiline output in Figure 2-9, you can see that there is a gap on either side of the columns. You can remove this gap by using the **is-gapless** class in conjunction with the **columns** container element (Listing 2-8).

Listing 2-8. Using Gapless Class to Remove Default Gaps

```
<div class="columns is-gapless is-multiline">

        <div class="column is-2" style="background-color:
        #7CFC00;">
        cat ipsum dolor cat ipsum dolor sit amet, eos...
        </div>
```

```
<div class="column is-10" style="background-color:
#FFFF00;">
cat ipsum dolor cat ipsum dolor sit amet, eos...
</div>

<div class="column is-9" style="background-color:
#E0FFFF">
cat ipsum dolor cat ipsum dolor sit amet, eos...
</div>

<div class="column is-3" style="background-color:
#FFEBCD">
cat ipsum dolor cat ipsum dolor sit amet, eos...
</div>
```
```
</div>
```

The output code is displayed in Figure 2-10.

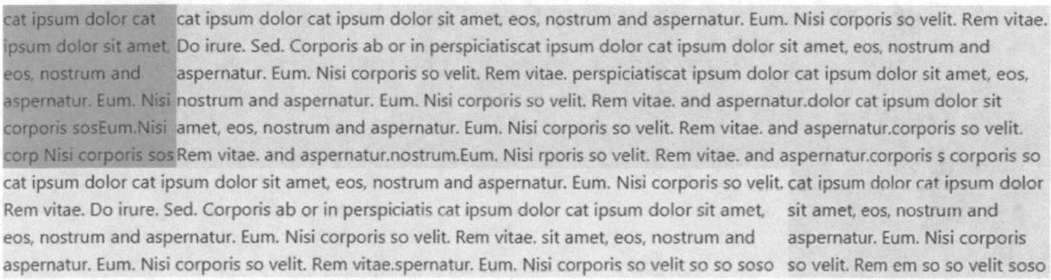

Figure 2-10. *Gapless columns*

On comparing Figure 2-10 with Figure 2-9 *(both have the same content and code except for the implemented gapless class in the latter screenshot)*, there is no gap between the columns in Figure 2-10.

Nested Columns

Nesting of columns is quite easy in Bulma. Let's see how it works with an example, as shown in Listing 2-9.

Listing 2-9. Nested Columns Code Structure

```
<div class="columns">
      <div class="column">
      <p style="background-color: Gainsboro">cat ipsum dolor
      sit amet, eos, nostrum amet, sos em... </p>
   <div class="columns is-mobile">
     <div class="column">
       <p style="background-color: Wheat"> cat ipsum dolor sit
       amet, eos, nostrum eoeamet, sos em... </p>
     </div>
     <div class="column">
       <p style="background-color: Gold"> cat ipsum dolor sit
       amet, eos, nostrum eoeamet, sos em... </p>
     </div>
   </div>
  </div>
</div>
```

As you see in Listing 2-9, we use the columns container. Then, we define a main element with the **column** class inside the main container and give a background *Gainsboro* color to the element. Next, we define a second container inside the preceding column using the **columns** container class, and we also assign an **is-mobile** class so that it shows the nested output design even on the mobile screen interface.

Next, we define two columns within the secondary container and assign the *Wheat* and *Gold* colors to them.

The output of the code is shown in Figure 2-11. In The figure, you can see a gap between the nested secondary columns. This is a default feature and, if needed, can be removed using the **is-gapless** class for the secondary columns container, which includes the nested columns.

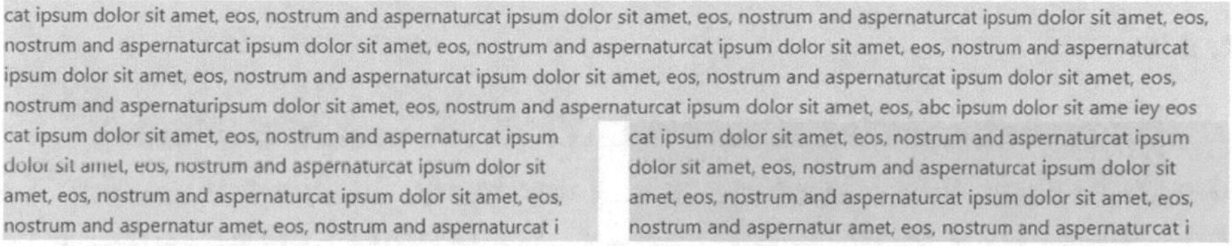

cat ipsum dolor sit amet, eos, nostrum and aspernaturcat ipsum dolor sit amet, eos, nostrum and aspernaturcat ipsum dolor sit amet, eos, nostrum and aspernaturcat ipsum dolor sit amet, eos, nostrum and aspernaturcat ipsum dolor sit amet, eos, nostrum and aspernaturcat ipsum dolor sit amet, eos, nostrum and aspernaturcat ipsum dolor sit amet, eos, nostrum and aspernaturcat ipsum dolor sit amet, eos, nostrum and aspernaturipsum dolor sit amet, eos, nostrum and aspernaturcat ipsum dolor sit amet, eos, abc ipsum dolor sit ame iey eos cat ipsum dolor sit amet, eos, nostrum and aspernaturcat ipsum   cat ipsum dolor sit amet, eos, nostrum and aspernaturcat ipsum dolor sit amet, eos, nostrum and aspernaturcat ipsum dolor sit   dolor sit amet, eos, nostrum and aspernaturcat ipsum dolor sit amet, eos, nostrum and aspernaturcat ipsum dolor sit amet, eos,   amet, eos, nostrum and aspernaturcat ipsum dolor sit amet, eos, nostrum and aspernatur amet, eos, nostrum and aspernaturcat i   nostrum and aspernatur amet, eos, nostrum and aspernaturcat i

Figure 2-11. *Nested columns*

The output with no gap between the nested columns is shown in Figure 2-12.

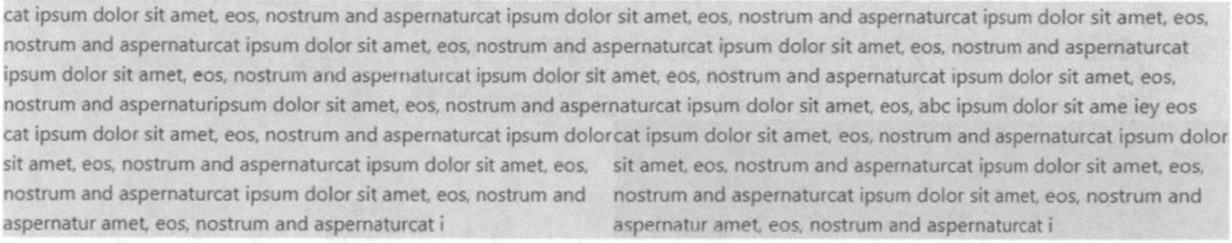

cat ipsum dolor sit amet, eos, nostrum and aspernaturcat ipsum dolor sit amet, eos, nostrum and aspernaturcat ipsum dolor sit amet, eos, nostrum and aspernaturcat ipsum dolor sit amet, eos, nostrum and aspernaturcat ipsum dolor sit amet, eos, nostrum and aspernaturcat ipsum dolor sit amet, eos, nostrum and aspernaturcat ipsum dolor sit amet, eos, nostrum and aspernaturipsum dolor sit amet, eos, nostrum and aspernaturcat ipsum dolor sit amet, eos, abc ipsum dolor sit ame iey eos cat ipsum dolor sit amet, eos, nostrum and aspernaturcat ipsum dolor cat ipsum dolor sit amet, eos, nostrum and aspernaturcat ipsum dolor sit amet, eos, nostrum and aspernaturcat ipsum dolor sit amet, eos,   sit amet, eos, nostrum and aspernaturcat ipsum dolor sit amet, eos, nostrum and aspernaturcat ipsum dolor sit amet, eos, nostrum and   nostrum and aspernaturcat ipsum dolor sit amet, eos, nostrum and aspernatur amet, eos, nostrum and aspernaturcat i   aspernatur amet, eos, nostrum and aspernaturcat i

Figure 2-12. *Nested gapless columns*

Offsets

Offsets in Bulma help you move columns to the right, meaning you can push them for more spacing. Let's see a code example (Listing 2-10).

Listing 2-10. Offset Classes Pushing Columns to the Right

```
<div class="columns is-mobile">
        <div class="column is-half is-offset-one-quarter"
        style="background-color: #FFEBCD;">
        cat ipsum dolor sit amet, eos, nostrum so velit......
        </div>
</div>
```

```
<div class="columns is-mobile">
        <div class="column is-half is-offset-one-quarter">
        <a class="button is-success  is-medium"> Submit </a>
        <a class="button is-info is-medium"> Cancel </a>
        </div>
</div>
```

The preceding code defines a main container using the **columns** container class. Next, we define an element inside that container using the **column** class. To the same element, we add the **is-half** class so that it spans half the length of the 12-column sized grid in the same row. We append an i**s-offset-one-quarter** class to it so that it is offset by 1/4 of the default 12-column size grid, meaning the element is pushed to the right by an equivalent space of three columns.

(We can create another container below the main container and define colored buttons; we will get to that part later on.)

The output of the code is shown in Figure 2-13.

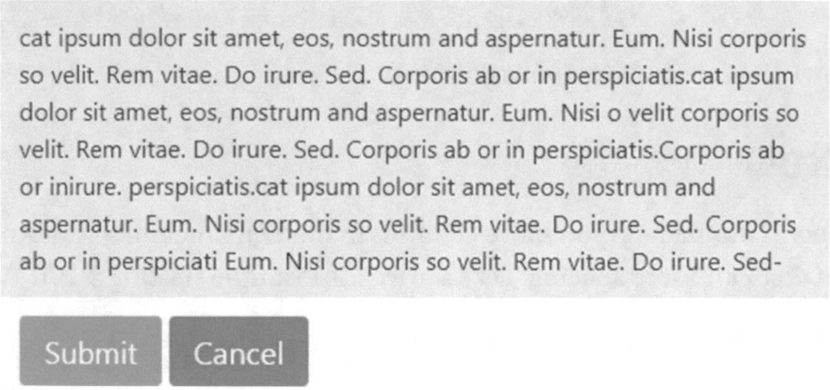

cat ipsum dolor sit amet, eos, nostrum and aspernatur. Eum. Nisi corporis so velit. Rem vitae. Do irure. Sed. Corporis ab or in perspiciatis.cat ipsum dolor sit amet, eos, nostrum and aspernatur. Eum. Nisi o velit corporis so velit. Rem vitae. Do irure. Sed. Corporis ab or in perspiciatis.Corporis ab or inirure. perspiciatis.cat ipsum dolor sit amet, eos, nostrum and aspernatur. Eum. Nisi corporis so velit. Rem vitae. Do irure. Sed. Corporis ab or in perspiciati Eum. Nisi corporis so velit. Rem vitae. Do irure. Sed-

Submit   Cancel

Figure 2-13. *Offset*

In the preceding screenshot, you can see that the element is offset by a quarter of the space assigned to a 12-column grid size.

To show the effect of the **is-pulled-left** and **is-pulled-right** classes, the **Submit** and **Cancel** buttons were added, wherein the classes were applied to them, respectively. By using these classes, the **Submit** button is pulled to the left and the **Cancel** button to the right of the container, respectively, as shown in Figure 2-14. (Refer to the last <div> element in Listing 2-10 code for the Submit and Cancel buttons)

cat ipsum dolor sit amet, eos, nostrum and aspernatur. Eum. Nisi corporis so velit. Rem vitae. Do irure. Sed. Corporis ab or in perspiciatis.cat ipsum dolor sit amet, eos, nostrum and aspernatur. Eum. Nisi o velit corporis so velit. Rem vitae. Do irure. Sed. Corporis ab or in perspiciatis.Corporis ab or inirure. perspiciatis.cat ipsum dolor sit amet, eos, nostrum and aspernatur. Eum. Nisi corporis so velit. Rem vitae. Do irure. Sed. Corporis ab or in perspiciati Eum. Nisi corporis so velit. Rem vitae. Do irure. Sed-

Submit   Cancel

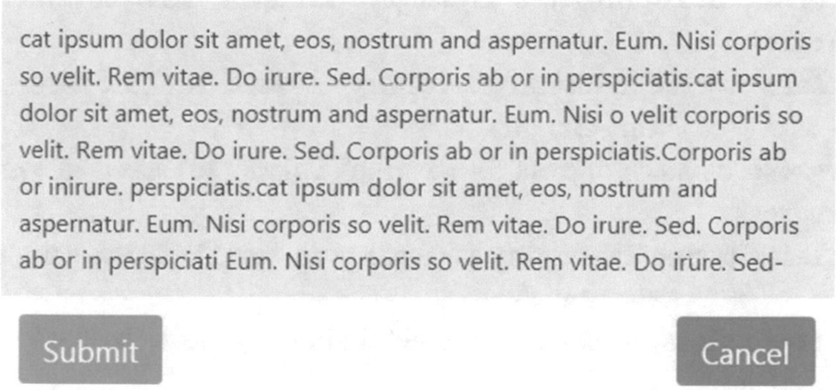

Figure 2-14. *Push and pull buttons*

Now that we took a look at the grids layout and the varied alternatives to define columns, we will move to Bulma's helper classes/utility classes in the next section.

Utility Classes

Utility classes are handy helpers that impact the styling of elements in the markup without using CSS style sheets. Since they are directly used in the markup, they speed up the work substantially. They are reusable and provide a high level of consistency in the code.

In this section, we will be discussing the color modifiers, responsive helpers, alignment helpers, and typography helpers baked into the Bulma framework.

Color Modifiers

Built-in color modifiers help render a certain color to the elements in Bulma.

Let's examine the functionality with a code example, as shown in Listing 2-11.

Listing 2-11. Bulma's Contextual Colors

```
<progress class="progress is-danger" value="5" max="80">10%
</progress>
<a class="button is-danger is-loading is-small"> Click Here </a>
             <br><br><br>
<progress class="progress is-warning" value="20" max="80">22%
</progress>
<a class="button is-warning is-loading is-small"> Click Here </a>
             <br><br><br>
<progress class="progress is-link" value="39" max="80">60%
</progress>
<a class="button is-link is-small"> Click Here </a>
             <br><br><br>
<progress class="progress is-success" value="65" max="80">83%
</progress>
<a class="button is-success is-small is-outlined"> Click Here
</a>
```

In the preceding code, we define four progress bars in this example; we create four *<progress>* elements and assign the **progress** class to each of them. Then we define the length parameters of the progress bars and the respective percentages w.r.t. of these progress bars. Under each progress bar, we add a button.

With each progress element we use a color helper class, namely **is-danger** class for the first progress bar as well as the button below it. Next, we assign the **is-warning** class to the second progress bar and the button below it.

Moving forward, we add different colors to the remaining *<progress>* elements and define colors and attributes to the buttons below it. (We have assigned a size class and the outlined shape as well as different status for the buttons, but we will learn about it further on in the book when we get to the buttons section.)

The output of the code is shown in Figure 2-15.

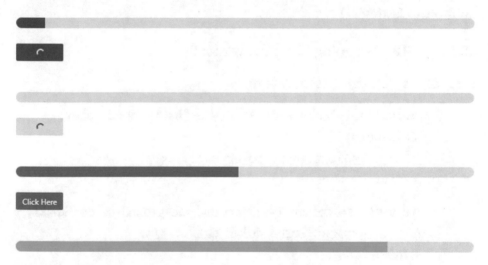

Figure 2-15. *Color helpers*

Alignment, Responsive, and Typography Helpers

This section deals with alignment, responsive, and typography utility elements. Initially, we will take a look at the alignment helper, followed by a code example for responsive helpers, and finally deal with the typography helpers,

Alignment Helper

Bulma can assign columns vertically, if necessary. All you need to do is assign the **is-vcentered** class to the columns. Let's see this in the code example in Listing 2-12.

Listing 2-12. Assigning Columns Vertically

```
<div class="columns is-vcentered">

        <div class="column is-7" style="background-color:
        Gainsboro;">
                <p>cat ipsum dolor cat ...</p>
        </div>

        <div class="column is-3" style="background-color: Khaki;">
                <p>cat ipsum dolor cat ...</p>
        </div>

</div>
```

In Listing 2-12 we assign the **is-vcentered** class to the columns container.

Then we create two column elements inside it and assign a different color to each of them.

The output of the code is seen in Figure 2-16.

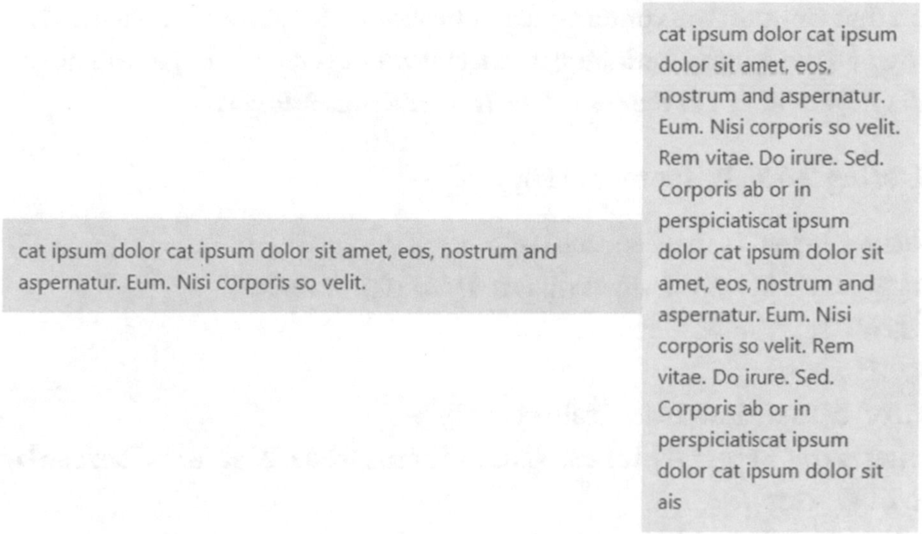

cat ipsum dolor cat ipsum dolor sit amet, eos, nostrum and aspernatur. Eum. Nisi corporis so velit.

cat ipsum dolor cat ipsum dolor sit amet, eos, nostrum and aspernatur. Eum. Nisi corporis so velit. Rem vitae. Do irure. Sed. Corporis ab or in perspiciatiscat ipsum dolor cat ipsum dolor sit amet, eos, nostrum and aspernatur. Eum. Nisi corporis so velit. Rem vitae. Do irure. Sed. Corporis ab or in perspiciatiscat ipsum dolor cat ipsum dolor sit ais

Figure 2-16. *Vertical column alignment*

Next, we discuss the responsive helpers.

Responsive Helpers

You can show/hide content depending on different-sized screens, namely, mobile phone, tablet, desktop, and widescreen.

In Listing 2-13 we use the **is-hidden-mobile** class for the first element, meaning the content will be shown in all devices apart from mobile screens. Then we insert an image within the first *<div>* element, using the image *<img>* tag.

Next, we create another *<div>* element and insert a different image; but here we use the **is-hidden-tablet-only** class, due to which the image can be seen on all screen-sizes except for tablet-sized screens. Moving forward, we create another *<div>* element and insert a different image; here we use the **is-hidden-desktop** class, meaning this image will be seen on a mobile as well as a tablet screen but will not be visible on desktop and larger than desktop screens. If we use the **only** attribute, it means that only on that viewport the content will not be visible. But if we do not use only, then all the screens pertaining to that viewport screen or larger will not be displayed (*except in the case of the **is-hidden-mobile** class*).

Listing 2-13. Responsive Helpers

```
<div class="is-hidden-mobile">
<img src="https://picsum.photos/id/1057/200/225"
alt="Altitude">
</div> <br>
<div class="is-hidden-tablet-only">
<img src="https://picsum.photos/id/1055/200/225" alt="Serene">
</div> <br>
<div class="is-hidden-desktop">
<img src="https://picsum.photos/id/1026/200/225" alt="Train">
</div>
```

The output of the code on mobile, tablet, and desktop screens, respectively, is shown in Figure 2-17.

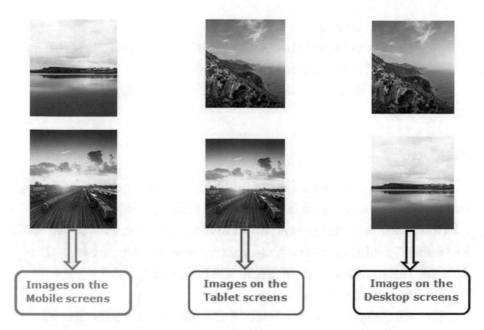

Figure 2-17. *Content responsively displayed on the mobile, tablet, and desktop screens*

Typography Helpers

Finally, let's look at typography helpers. They generally help us change the size and color of the text on multiple viewports (as defined at the breakpoints), if needed. Let's look at the code example in Listing 2-14.

Listing 2-14. Different Typography Utilities

```
<section class="section">
  <div class="container">
      <h1 class="title is-size-5-mobile has-text-centered-
      mobile is-size-3-tablet has-text-right-tablet-only
      is-size-1-desktop has-text-left-desktop is-uppercase
      has-text-success">
          Hello World!
      </h1>
```

```
            <br><br><br>
        <p class="subtitle is-italic has-text-weight-light is-
        capitalized has-text-link">
            Bulma---> awesome, rockin' & intuitive
        </p>
    </div>
</section>
```

In Listing 2-14, we use a *<section>* element as the container. Following this, we create a heading *<h1>* element and assign the **title** class to it.

Then, we define the size and position of the element. Initially we assign the **is-size-5-mobile** and **has-text-centered-mobile** classes to the *<h1>* element. This means that the element will be of **size 5** and the text will be centered on a mobile phone screen.

Next, we assign the **is-size-3-tablet** and **has-text-right-tablet-only** classes to the same *<h1>* element; this defines **size 3** for the text on a tablet and the alignment of the text to the right side of the screen on a tablet screen only.

Moving forward, we assign the **is-size-1-desktop** and **has-text-left-desktop** classes to the same *<h1>* element. This effectively assigns **size 1** to the text and aligns the text to the left on a desktop screen.

For more information related to text size, refer to Table 2-1.

Table 2-1. *Font Size Chart*

Class	Font-Size
is-size-1	3rem
is-size-2	2.5rem
is-size-3	2rem
is-size-4	1.5rem
is-size-5	1.25rem
is-size-6	1rem
is-size-7	0.75rem

Thereon, for the same *<h1>* element, the **is-uppercase** is applied, thereby rendering the text in uppercase text. Then, we finally apply the **has-text-success** class to the same element for it to display the respective green color.

Now that we have applied all these classes to the *<h1>* element, we will move on to create a paragraph *<p>* element. We apply the **subtitle** class followed by the **is-italic** class, which will apply the typography style and display the text in italics. Later on, we use the **has-text-weight-light** class to it for defining the font-weight. Finally, we use the **is-capitalized** and **has-text-link** classes, due to which the text is shown in capitalized case with the blue link color.

The output of the code on a mobile screen is shown in Figure 2-18.

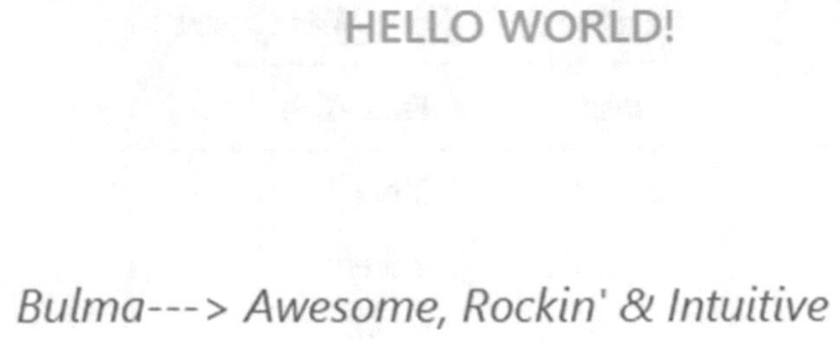

HELLO WORLD!

Bulma---> Awesome, Rockin' & Intuitive

Figure 2-18. *Content displayed on a mobile screen*

From Figure 2-18, you can see that the **Hello World!** text is in uppercase and centered on the mobile screen. The size (*size-5*) and color are also displayed as defined in the code.

Similarly, when you see the same output on a tablet screen it is different, as shown in Figure 2-19.

HELLO WORLD!

Bulma---> Awesome, Rockin' & Intuitive

Figure 2-19. *Content displayed on a tablet screen*

As you can see from the preceding screenshot, the Hello World! text is aligned to the right on a tablet screen. You can also see the difference in the font-size (*size-3*) as defined in the code. In Figure 2-20, the Hello World! text is aligned to the left on a desktop screen. You can also see the bigger font-size (*size-1*) as defined in the code.

HELLO WORLD!

Bulma---> Awesome, Rockin' & Intuitive

Figure 2-20. *Content displayed on a desktop screen*

Finally, you can also the text ***Bulma---> Awesome, Rockin' & Intuitive*** text in capitalized case with italics styling on all three screens as per the defined markup.

Summary

In this chapter, we looked at various grid features, including columns, offsets, gaps, and other different ways of styling columns. We also looked at the utility helpers and modifiers that are quite handy in web design and also speed up your website significantly. In the next chapter, we will look at in-depth content and code for the Layout CSS helpers in Bulma, such as *tiles*, *box elements*, *media objects*, and *cards,* to mention a few. So, stay tuned for more.

CHAPTER 3

Layout CSS Helpers

In modern layouts, texts are not placed in an ad-hoc way compared to the archaic ways used in old, legacy web sites. Containers are an awesome control for placing and grouping text, images, graphics, headings, buttons, and glyphicons in a single group.

It is quite handy, as you can resize, move, adjust, modify, or place the entire container group instead of moving each individual element inside it. Containers, levels, media objects, banners, tiles, cards, boxes, and panels are the various containers in Bulma that help enclose different types of content within it.

In this chapter, we will look at these Bulma containers, which are quite useful in modern layouts in this digital era. Let's get started right away.

Containers and Levels

In Bulma, the container control centers the content horizontally. In addition, Bulma's container element is responsive and brings out a certain consistency across different devices, specifically tailored for mobile platforms.

In Listing 3-1, we will learn how to use the container element. However, we will first define the columns grid container and then create a separate container control, to show the difference between the grid columns container and the separate container control.

© Aravind Shenoy 2020
A. Shenoy, *Learning Bulma*, https://doi.org/10.1007/978-1-4842-5482-0_3

Listing 3-1. Grid Container vs. Standalone Container Element

```
<div class="columns">

  <div class="is-mobile is-centered" style="border:5px solid
  OliveDrab;">
        <div class="column is-full"  style="background-color:
        Wheat;">
        <p>
        cat ipsum dolor sit amet...
        </p>
        </div>
  </div>
  </div>
  <br> <br> <br>

  <div class="section" style="border:5px solid OliveDrab;">
    <div class="container" style="background-color: Wheat;">
     <p>
        cat ipsum dolor sit amet, ....
      </p>
    </div>
  </div>
</div>
```

In Listing 3-1, we define the columns grid, which is centered. We use the ***is-full*** class for the columns so that it occupies all 12 columns of the grid. We assign a border and wheat color to it.

Then we create an independent container element using the container class. We assign a border and wheat color to it just like we did for the columns container.

The output of the code is shown in Figure 3-1.

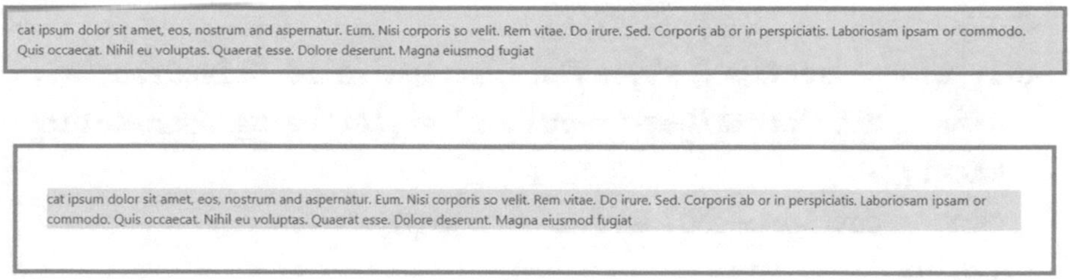

cat ipsum dolor sit amet, eos, nostrum and aspernatur. Eum. Nisi corporis so velit. Rem vitae. Do irure. Sed. Corporis ab or in perspiciatis. Laboriosam ipsam or commodo. Quis occaecat. Nihil eu voluptas. Quaerat esse. Dolore deserunt. Magna eiusmod fugiat

cat ipsum dolor sit amet, eos, nostrum and aspernatur. Eum. Nisi corporis so velit. Rem vitae. Do irure. Sed. Corporis ab or in perspiciatis. Laboriosam ipsam or commodo. Quis occaecat. Nihil eu voluptas. Quaerat esse. Dolore deserunt. Magna eiusmod fugiat

Figure 3-1. *Grid column full width vs. normal container*

As you can see in Figure 3-1, the output varies. The initial output container is the 12-grid columns container, while the container below is designed with the container class. You can see the space and padding around the content, which results in a different output compared with the 12-column full-width grid layout.

Even the container element in Bulma comes in regular, full width, and widescreen sizes. For a full HD screen, all you need to do is add the ***is-fullhd*** class to the container class. In Listing 3-2, we have just added the ***is-fullhd*** class to the container class from the previous code Listing 3-1.

Listing 3-2. Grid Column Full Width vs. Full HD Container

```
<div class="is-mobile is-centered" style="border:5px solid
OliveDrab;">
        <div class="column is-full"  style="background-color:
        Wheat;">
        <p> cat ipsum dolor... </p>
        </div>
  </div>
  </div>
  <br> <br> <br>
```

```
<body>
<div class="section" style="border:5px solid OliveDrab;">
  <div class="container is-fullhd" style="background-color:
  Wheat;">
    <p>   cat ipsum dolor....      </p>
  </div>
</div>
```

The output of the code is seen in Figure 3-2.

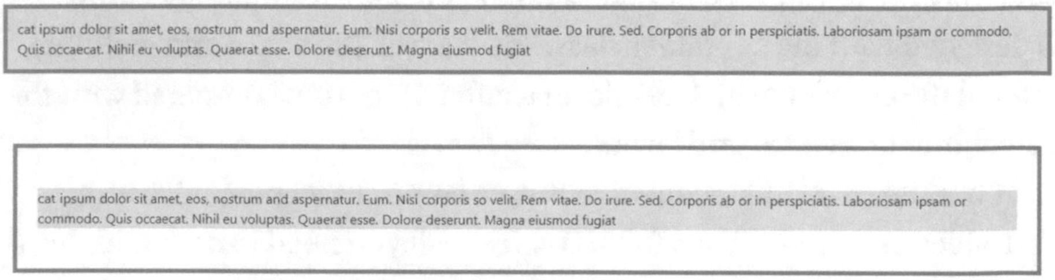

Figure 3-2. *Grid column full width vs. full HD container*

The full HD container is wider; therefore, the content is stretched to the right and left occupying more space due to the is-fullhd class.

To see the difference between a normal container and a full HD container more clearly, let's see the code in Listing 3-3.

Listing 3-3. Normal Standalone Container vs. Full HD Container Component

```
<div class="section" style="border:3px solid OliveDrab;">
  <div class="container" style="background-color: Wheat;">
    <p>
      cat ipsum dolor...
    </p>
  </div>
    </div>
```

```
<br>
<div class="section" style="border:3px solid
OliveDrab;">
<div class="container is-fullhd" style="background-color:
Wheat;">
 <p>
    cat ipsum dolor...
  </p>
</div>
        </div>
        <br>
</div>
```

The output of the code is seen in Figure 3-3.

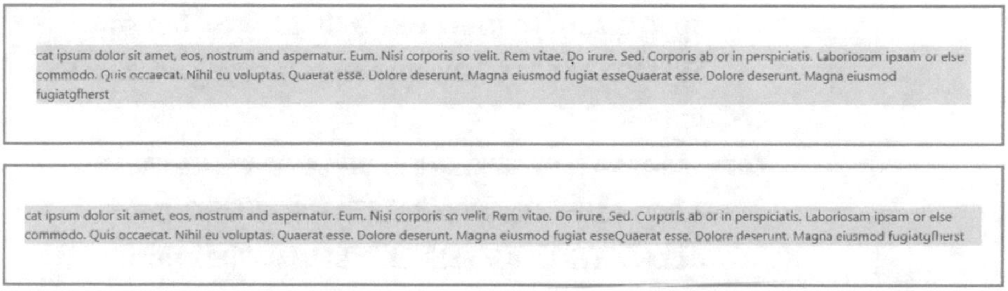

cat ipsum dolor sit amet, eos, nostrum and aspernatur. Eum. Nisi corporis so velit. Rem vitae. Do irure. Sed. Corporis ab or in perspiciatis. Laboriosam ipsam or else commodo. Quis occaecat. Nihil eu voluptas. Quaerat esse. Dolore deserunt. Magna eiusmod fugiat esseQuaerat esse. Dolore deserunt. Magna eiusmod fugiatgfherst

cat ipsum dolor sit amet, eos, nostrum and aspernatur. Eum. Nisi corporis so velit. Rem vitae. Do irure. Sed. Corporis ab or in perspiciatis. Laboriosam ipsam or else commodo. Quis occaecat. Nihil eu voluptas. Quaerat esse. Dolore deserunt. Magna eiusmod fugiat esseQuaerat esse. Dolore deserunt. Magna eiusmod fugiatgfherst

Figure 3-3. *Normal container control vs. full HD container*

In Figure 3-3, you can see the normal container element followed by that of the full HD container element. You can now clearly see the difference between the normal and full HD container, as the content occupies more space to the right and left of the viewport for the full HD element (remember that the content is the same for both these containers).

Bulma also has a levels container, which can be used for most of the web site's elements. The difference between levels and container control is that the elements within the levels control are centered vertically by default.

Let's look at the code for the levels container in Listing 3-4.

Listing 3-4. Levels Container Element

```
<div class="section" style="border:3px solid YellowGreen;">
    <div class="container">
            <nav class="level">
            <div class="level-left">
                    <p class="level-item"><a class="button
                    is-primary"><strong> Bulma Mail</strong></a>
                    </p>
                    <p class="level-item"><a class="button
                    is-info"><strong>Compose</strong></a></p>
                    <p class="level-item"><a class="button
                    is-info"><strong>Delete</strong></a></p>
                    <p class="level-item"><a class="button
                    is-success"><strong>Send</strong></a></p>
            </div>
            <div class="level-item has-text-centered">
                    <img src="Images/MATRIX-OF-SHREK.png"
                    alt="MATRIX-OF-SHREK" style="height:
                    175px;">
            </div>
            <div class="level-right">
                <div class="level-item">
                  <div class="field has-addons">
                      <p class="control">
                        <input class="input" type="text"
                        placeholder="Enter Search Item">
                      </p>
```

```
            <p class="control">
              <button class="button">
                  <strong>Search</strong>
              </button>
            </p>
          </div>
        </div>
      </div>
      </nav>
  </div>
</div>
```

In Listing 3-4, we used the container element for an element. Inside the column of the container, we created a `<nav>` tag to which we assigned the *level* class. Moving forward, we create a `<div>` element to which we assign the *level-left* class. This will align the element to the left of the container. We create four paragraph `<p>` elements with the level-item class. We include links within each `<p>` tag and design button for each link using the *button* class. We use different contextual colors for each of the four buttons: primary, link, info, and success.

Next, we create another `<div>` element and assign a *level-item* class to it and include the *has-text-centered* class. This will align the content in the center of the levels container. We also include an image inside this `<div>` element, which is also centered.

Further, we create the third `<div>` element and assign the *level-right* class to it. Then we define a *level-item* class for a `<div>` element inside the third `<div>`element. We create a search box. Initially, for creating the search box we define a `<div>` and assign the *field* class to it. Then we create a paragraph element `<p>` and assign the *control* class to it. We then use the *input* class with the type as text and include a placeholder. Next, we create the Search button. For this we add the *has-addons* class to the *field* class, using which we had created the search box. Now we create a button element below the <p> tag and assign the same *control* class to it. Then we name the button as Search.

The output of the code is shown in Figure 3-4.

Figure 3-4. *Levels container*

As you can see, the *level-left* class has pulled the content to the left, whereas the *level-right* class has pushed the content to the right of the levels container.

Media Objects

Social media web sites usually have text next to several graphical formats such as images, icons, infographics, or videos. Media objects help you in designing this structure, wherein data or information is placed alongside graphical content in a hassle-free, uncomplicated manner. This UI component is quite handy in repetitive design like blog posts, comments, tweets, etc.

Bulma's media objects can be better understood by the following code:

Listing 3-5. Media Object with Image and Content

```
<article class="media">
  <figure class="media-left">
    <img src="Images/Shrek.png" alt="Shrek-In-Matrix"
    style="height: 93px;">
  </figure>
```

```
<div class="media-content">
  <div class="content">
    <p>
      <strong>Shrek</strong>
      <br>
       Havana brown. Malkin...
      <br>
      <small><a><strong>Love it :- <span class="icon is-
      small"><i class="fas fa-heart"></i></span></strong>
      </a> ········ <a> <strong>Reply all :-<span class="icon
      is-small"><i class="fas fa-reply"></i></span></
      strong></a> ········  <strong>3 days</strong> </small>
    </p>
  </div>
</article>
```

In Listing 3-5, we defined a main <article> tag to which we assign a *media* class. Then, we use the <figure> tag to which we assign the ***media-left*** class and insert an image source using the <img> tag. After the media is defined, we create a <div> element within the main <article> tag below the <figure> tag and assign the ***media-content*** class to it. Then we create another element inside it, assign the ***content*** class, and enter the sample prose. Once the sample prose has been entered, we define the three icons below it using the Bulma supported icon tags (we will get to icons in later chapters). See Figure 3-5.

Figure 3-5. *Main media object with the image and the content*

Moving forward, we will nest a text area below this media object as seen in Listing 3-6.

Listing 3-6. Adding a Text Area Box

```
<article class="media">
            <div class="media-content">
                <div class="field">
                  <p class="control">
                        <textarea class="textarea"
                        placeholder="What are you
                        thinking....post here"></textarea>
                  </p>
                </div>
                <div class="field">
                  <p class="control">
                        <button class="button is-
                        success">Submit comment</button>
                  </p>
                </div>
            </div>
        </article>
        <br>
    </article>
```

In Listing 3-6, we nest a text area akin to the one seen in a form. This text area will be nested inside the main <article> tag used at the first line of code in Listing 3-5. For designing the text area, again we use an <article> tag (think child article), and assign the *media* class to it. Since there is no image in the text area code, we directly use a <div> element and assign the *media-content* class to it. Then we create a paragraph element and assign the *control* class to it. We define a text area element with the *textarea* class. Below the textarea element, we define another <div> and assign the *field* class to it. Next we define a paragraph tag and assign the same *control* class to it as the one used in the text area code. Then we create a button using the button element and assign the **is-success** contextual color to it (the color is similar to spring green and is a built-in contextual color.

The output of the code so far is seen in Figure 3-6.

Figure 3-6. *Text area below the main media object*

Following this, we nest a media object below the text area, as seen in Listing 3-7.

Listing 3-7. Nested Media Object Below the Parent Media Object

```
<article class="media">
                <figure class="media-left">
  <img src="Images/Oracle.png" alt="Oracle" style="height:
  93px;">
  </figure>
                <div class="media-content">
                    <div class="content">
                      <p>
                            <strong> ORACLE </strong>
                            <br>
                            Malkin scottish fold....
```

```
                    <br>
                    <small><a><strong>Love it :- <span
                    class="icon is-small"><i class="fas
                    fa-heart"></i></span></strong>
        </a> ········   <a> <strong>Reply all :- <span
        class="icon is-small"><i class="fas fa-reply">
        </i></span></strong></a> ········   <strong> 1
        day</strong> </small>
            </p>
          </div>
        </div>
      </article>
```

In Listing 3-7, we define a nested <article> element. We assign the *media* class to it. Then we use a <figure> tag to which we assign the *media-left* class. Next we insert an image using the <img> tag. Then we define a <div> to which we assign the *media-content* class. Next, we define a <div> element within the preceding <div> element and assign the *content* class to it. The code is same as the one when we created the first media object except that this is a nested article tag and the sample image and content are different.

The output of the code so far is shown in Figure 3-7.

Shrek
Havana brown. Malkin. Ragdoll tomcat but mouser british shorthair for russian blue. Manx munchkin. Panther birman so tom so kittenklp himalayan yet egyptian mau. Bobcat bobcat jaguar Egyptian mau maine coonblue. Manx munchkin. Panther birman so
Love it :- ♥ ⸺ Reply all :-↰ ⸺ **3 days**

What are you thinking....post here

Submit comment

NEO
Cat ipsum dolor sit amet, manx. Sphynx. Matrix revolutions reloaded tabby but lynx yet american shorthair. Havana brown siames fhre
Love it :- ♥ ⸺ Reply all :- ↰ ⸺ **7hrs**

Figure 3-7. *Nested media object under the text area*

Then we create another media object in a similar manner. The code for the next media object is shown in Listing 3-8.

Listing 3-8. Adding the Other Nested Media Object

```
<article class="media">
                <figure class="media-left">
  <img src="Images/Oracle.png" alt="Oracle" style="height:
  93px;">
  </figure>
                <div class="media-content">
                    <div class="content">
                      <p>
                            <strong> ORACLE </strong>
                            <br>
                            Malkin scottish fold. Singapura
                            abyssinian kitty and manx balinese .
                            Tiger manx so norwegian forest but
                            british shorthair. Mouser xega

                            <br>
                            <small><a><strong>Love it :- <span
                            class="icon is-small"><i class="fas
                            fa-heart"></i></span></strong>
        </a> ········  <a> <strong>Reply all :- <span
        class="icon is-small"><i class="fas fa-reply">
        </i></span></strong></a> <strong> 1 day</strong>
        </small>
                    </p>
                  </div>
                </div>
              </article>
```

The output of the entire code is shown in Figure 3-8.

Shrek
Havana brown. Malkin. Ragdoll tomcat but mouser british shorthair for russian blue. Manx munchkin. Panther birman so tom so kittenklp himalayan yet egyptian mau. Bobcat bobcat jaguar Egyptian mau maine coonblue. Manx munchkin. Panther birman so
Love it :- ♥ ⋯⋯ Reply all :- ↩ ⋯⋯ 3 days

What are you thinking...post here

Submit comment

NEO
Cat ipsum dolor sit amet, manx. Sphynx. Matrix revolutions reloaded tabby but lynx yet american shorthair. Havana brown siames fhre
Love it :- ♥ ⋯⋯ Reply all :- ↩ ⋯⋯ 7hrs

ORACLE
Malkin scottish fold. Singapura abyssinian kitty and manx balinese . Tiger manx so norwegian forest but british shorthair. Mouser xega
Love it :- ♥ ⋯⋯ Reply all :- ↩ ⋯⋯ 1 day

Figure 3-8. *Entire media object code output*

Banners

The Hero banner is a UI component in Bulma used to highlight the site's most essential content. Hero banners draw user attention, making it useful from a saleable aspect in modern web site layouts, akin to traditional banners and posters in traditional advertising.

In line with the "pictures speak louder than words" viewpoint, Hero banners help in products/solutions promotion on web sites. Bulma's Hero banners help add images and aesthetical content, well suited for those web layouts where there is usually minimal data, prevalent in single page design.

To understand banners really well, let's see an example in Listing 3-9.

Listing 3-9. Basic Hero Banner

```
<section class="hero">
  <div class="hero-body">
    <div class="container">
      <h1 class="title">
        Banner Main Title
      </h1>
      <h2 class="subtitle">
        Banner Subtitle
      </h2>
    </div>
  </div>
</section>
```

In Listing 3-9, we have used a section tag and assigned a ***hero*** class to it. The `<div>` within the `<section>` tag has been assigned the ***hero-body*** class. We create another `<div>` with the container class and then define the title and subtitle for the Hero banner.

The output of the code is shown in Figure 3-9.

Banner Main Title
Banner Subtitle

Figure 3-9. *Basic Hero banner*

We can add contextual colors to the banner. We need to add the specific contextual color class to the `<section>` tag to which the ***hero*** class is assigned. Let's see an example where we have assigned the contextual color success (a shade of green) to it.

Listing 3-10. Creating a Hero Banner with a Contextual Color

```
<section class="hero is-success">
  <div class="hero-body">
    <div class="container">
      <h1 class="title">
        Banner Main Title
      </h1>
      <h2 class="subtitle">
        Banner Subtitle
      </h2>
    </div>
  </div>
</section>
```

The output of the code is shown in Figure 3-10.

Banner Main Title
Banner Subtitle

Figure 3-10. *Success contextual color for the Hero banner*

You can establish a gradient feel to any color by adding the ***is-bold*** class in conjunction with the color class of the banner. You can also define difference sizes for the banner by using the respective medium, large, and fullheight classes. Let's see an example in Listing 3-11, where we have used the gradient bold class and the fullheight class alongside the hero class.

Listing 3-11. Adding a Gradient to Contextual Color Alongside the Fullheight Attribute

```
<section class="hero is-bold is-success is-fullheight">
  <div class="hero-body">
    <div class="container">
      <h1 class="title">
        Banner Main Title
      </h1>
      <h2 class="subtitle">
        Banner Subtitle
      </h2>
    </div>
  </div>
</section>
```

The output of this code is shown in Figure 3-11.

Figure 3-11. *Hero banner with the success color gradient and fullheight size*

In a full-height Hero banner, we can define the navigation in the top section by using the ***hero-head*** class. Then we can define the banner body by using the ***hero-body*** class. Finally, we can design the footer of the Hero banner using the ***hero-foot*** class.

Let's understand it by means of the example in Listing 3-12.

Listing 3-12. Hero Head and Body Code

```
<section class="hero is-bold is-primary is-fullheight">
 <!-- Banner Top -->
 <br>
 <div class="hero-head">
    <div class="container">
        <nav class="breadcrumb is-centered">
  <ul>
    <li><a href="#" class="has-text-white">Home</a></li>
    <li><a href="#" class="has-text-white">About</a></li>
    <li><a href="#" class="has-text-white">Portfolio</a></li>
      <li><a href="#" class="has-text-white">Services</a></li>
    <li><a href="#" class="has-text-white">Blogs</a></li>
  </ul>
</nav>
    </div>
      </div>
  <!-- Banner Body -->
  <div class="hero-body">
    <div class="container">
      <h1 class="title has-text-centered">
        Shrek Solutions
      </h1>
```

```
    <h2 class="subtitle has-text-centered">
      Web Matrix Architecture
      </h2>
    </div>
  </div>
  </nav>
  </div>
</section>
```

In Listing 3-12, we have defined the code for the Hero head and Hero body sections. Initially, we use the code for creating a full-height banner. We assign the *hero*, *is-bold*, *is-primary*, and *is-fullheight* classes to the <section> tag. The banner therefore is a full-height hero banner with a gradient color shade of the primary contextual color.

Then we define the enclosed <div> with the *hero-head* class. Within this we include another <div> element and assign the *container* class to it, to create a container-based padded layout. Then we use a <nav> navigation element and assign the *breadcrumb* class to create a navigation breadcrumb. We further use the *is-centered* class to the <nav> element so that the breadcrumb is positioned at the center in the hero-head section.

Moving forward, we create an unordered list using the <ul> tag and the <li> tags within the <ul> tags. Once we have defined the name of the navigation options, we move on to the body section of the banner.

In the banner body section, we create a separate <div> element and assign the *hero-body* class to it. We define a container for the body section using the *container* class for the enclosed <div> element. We define the headings using the title and subtitle classes. Once we code the names of the headings, we move on to executing this part of the code.

The output of the code so far is shown in Figure 3-12.

Figure 3-12. *Hero banner head and body sections*

Then, we proceed to creating the footer section of the Hero banner. The code is shown in Listing 3-13.

Listing 3-13. Adding the Footer Section

```
<div class="hero-foot">
    <nav class="tabs is-boxed is-fullwidth">
      <div class="container">
        <ul>
          <li>
            <a class="socicon-sharethis" style="border:2px
            solid White;"></a>
          </li>
          <li>
            <a class="socicon-facebook" style="border:2px solid
            White;"></a>
          </li>
```

```
<li>
  <a class="socicon-twitter" style="border:2px solid
  White;"></a>
</li>
<li>
  <a class="socicon-snapchat" style="border:2px solid
  White;"></a>
</li>
<li>
  <a class="socicon-pinterest" style="border:2px
  solid White;"></a>
</li>
<li>
  <a class="socicon-linkedin" style="border:2px solid
  White;"></a>
</li>
<li>
  <a class="socicon-youtube" style="border:2px solid
  White;"></a>
</li>
 <li>
  <a class="socicon-whatsapp" style="border:2px solid
  White;"></a>
</li>
 <li>
  <a class="socicon-tumblr" style="border:2px solid
  White;"></a>
</li>
<li>
  <a class="socicon-mail" style="border:2px solid
  White;"></a>
</li>
```

```
        </ul>
      </div>
    </nav>
  </div>
```

As you can see from the preceding code, we first create a separate
<div> element, to which we assign the *hero-foot* class. Then we enclose
a <nav> tag inside it and add the *tabs* class to create a navigation element
at the bottom in the footer. We design the box for the footer and give it
complete width using the *is-boxed* and *is-fullwidth* classes. Next, we
create a container control using the *container* class. Inside the container,
we create an unordered list and include the various list items using the
<ul> and <li> tags. To those items, we assign the link using the <a> tag for
each list item. We then assign a white border to those list items. You will
observe that we used the **socicon** classes for each social media icon in the
<li> tags.

For this, we have used the icons from the free Socicon web site at the
following web address:

www.socicon.com

Note   For this example, we have used the Socicon CDN link on AWS
servers in the <head> section of the Hero banner code along with the
CDN link for Bulma CSS. Without adding the CDN link for Socicon, the
code will not work; so make sure you include it in the <head> section.

```
<link rel="stylesheet" href="https://s3.amazonaws.com/icomoon.
io/114779/Socicon/style.css?u8vidh">
```

After adding the respective socicon class (based on different social
media icons), we can now see the final output in Figure 3-13.

Figure 3-13. *Full-height hero banner breadcrumb navigation &*
footer

As you can see, we have a full-height Hero banner with a breadcrumb
navigation and a footer with several social media icons and other buttons
like Share and Mail, to name a few.

Cards and Tiles

Cards are UI controls that help incorporate relevant information such as
titles, user names, images, icons, and call-to-action buttons uniformly in
a card format. All this data is shown with visuals on an equal pane. The
flexibility and modular approach is prevalent across different sites like
news postings, Tinder interfaces, and pictures seen under the Images tab
in Google search, to name a few.

The card format delivers substantial information in a compact
way with proper whitespace usage. It can also be used to group similar
information in a consistent format across all viewpoints, ranging from
desktops to mobile phones. For example, on an e-commerce site,
information related to a specific genre of products is displayed in different

rectangular cards along with their respective images with the same call-to-action functionality.

UI/UX designers promote the use of card-like design for its interactive and user-satisfying capabilities, as they can make effective use of the whitespace and deliver information in a compact form without clutter or noise. Moreover, cards demonstrate excellent responsiveness across all device or screen sizes, thereby bringing ultimate consistency and flexibility to your web site designing projects. Bulma also has an ingrained tile component, which is a card-like, metro-style container—a design previously observed in legacy Windows phones (think circa 2008–2010). Known as flat-and-modular design, it provides a high degree of readability of text and visuals, apart from ensuring a satisfying and interactive user experience across all breakpoints.

Let's explore cards and tiles using simple examples. Initially we will see an example of cards before proceeding to tiles.

For the cards component, we will be using the *card* class. The *card-image* class is for images to be used in the card. The *card-content* class is for the titles and subtitles for the card and other text. For the footer, Bulma uses the *card-footer* class.

Listing 3-14. Creating a Basic Card and Adding an Image

```
<div class="card">
    <div class="card-image">
    <figure class="image is-130x150">
      <img src="Images/Coffee-Shop-PixaBay.png" alt="Coffee-
      Shop-PixaBay">
    </figure>
    </div>
  </div>
```

In Listing 3-14, we define a main `<div>` and use the card class with it. Then, we create another `<div>` element and assign the card-image class to it. Then, using the `<figure>` element, we insert an image source in the `<img>` tag.

The output of the code is shown in Figure 3-14.

Figure 3-14. *Image for the card on a mobile screen*

Below the image, we define the card content. We create a `<div>` element and assign the ***card-content*** class to it. We assign a title and subtitle with different heading tags, using the title and subtitle class. Whereas we assign the ***is-4*** class text size for the title, we use ***is-7*** class text size for the subtitle. We also define a light grey color to the subtitle text using the ***has-text-grey-light*** class. Refer to Listing 3-15.

Listing 3-15. Adding Content to the Image

```
<div class="card-content">
      <p class="title is-4">SHREK CAFE</p>
        <p class="subtitle is-7 has-text-grey-light"> Italian &
        American Coffee</p>
      <div class="content is-size-6">
      European-influenced coffee shop for international snacks
      and coffee drinks using espresso bases
      </div>
   </div>
   <p class="card-header-title">
     <b> Reservation--> Book Now </b>
   </p>
```

The output of the card on a mobile screen after adding the content is shown in Figure 3-15.

SHREK CAFE
Italian & American Coffee

European-influenced coffee shop
for international snacks and coffee
drinks using espresso bases

Reservation--> Book Now

Figure 3-15. Card with the content and image

Then we define the footer for the card using the footer tags as shown in Listing 3-16:

Listing 3-16. Defining the Footer for the Card

```
<footer class="card-footer">
    <a href="#" class="card-footer-item"><b> 5:00 PM </b></a>
    <a href="#" class="card-footer-item"><b> 7:00 PM </b></a>
    <a href="#" class="card-footer-item"><b> 9:00 PM </b></a>
  </footer>
```

```
<footer class="card-footer">
  <a href="#" class="card-footer-item"> <span class="icon
  is-large"><i class="fas fa-envelope fa-2x"></i> </span>
  </a>
  <a href="#" class="card-footer-item"> <span class="icon
  is-large"><i class="fas fa-share-alt-square fa-2x"></i>
  </span></a>
  <a href="#" class="card-footer-item"> <span class="icon
  is-large"><i class="fas fa-comments fa-2x"></i> </span>
  </a>
<br>
</footer>
<footer class="card-footer">
 <a href="#" class="card-footer-item"> <span class="socicon-
 facebook"></span> </a>
   <a href="#" class="card-footer-item"> <span
   class="socicon-twitter"></span> </a>
   <a href="#" class="card-footer-item"> <span
   class="socicon-snapchat"></span> </a>
  <a href="#" class="card-footer-item"> <span class="socicon-
  pinterest"></span> </a>
   <a href="#" class="card-footer-item"> <span
   class="socicon-linkedin"></span> </a>
<br>
</footer>
```

In Listing 3-16, we create three <footer> elements. For each <footer> tag, we use the *card-footer* class.

In the first <footer> element, we create three links and assign the *card-footer-item* classes to them. We then jot down the booking timings as 5:00 p.m., 7:00 p.m., and 9:00 p.m.

In the second <footer> element, we create three links and assign the ***card-footer-item*** class to three items. However, we define the Font Awesome icons for Mail, Share, and Comments. We also increase the size of the icons by using the ***icon is-large*** and the exponential ***fa-2x*** classes for them.

In the third <footer> element, we create three links and assign the ***card-footer-item*** class to each of them. We then use the Socicon links for the five social media sites (Facebook, Twitter, Snapchat, Pinterest, and LinkedIn).

The output of the complete code is seen in Figure 3-16.

Figure 3-16. *Card with the content, image, and footer*

In Figure 3-16, we can see the entire card we have created for Shrek Café.

Now, we look at the flat-design tile element. We define the tile by using the *tile* class with an element. In Bulma, the tiles have a particular hierarchy. Initially, the hierarchy is as follows:

```
tile is-ancestor
|
|---------tile is-parent
       |
       |--------- tile is-child
```

The **is-ancestor** class is the highest followed by the **is-parent** class, which in turn is followed by **is-child,** which is the lowest in the hierarchy. You can also nest tiles deeper than that. Following is the hierarchy for deeper child elements within connecting parent elements:

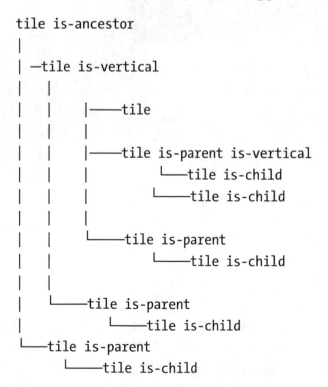

```
tile is-ancestor
|
| —tile is-vertical
|   |
|   |     |——tile
|   |     |
|   |     |——tile is-parent is-vertical
|   |     |        └——tile is-child
|   |     |        └——tile is-child
|   |     |
|   |     └——tile is-parent
|   |              └——tile is-child
|   |
|   └——tile is-parent
|            └——tile is-child
└——tile is-parent
         └——tile is-child
```

Let's further understand this using a code example.

Listing 3-17. Creating Basic Tiles

```
<div class="tile is-ancestor">
  <div class="tile is-8 is-parent">
    <div class="tile is-4 is-child box">
      <p class="title">Column Ia</p>
      <p>Cat ipsum dolor ...amet </p>
    </div>
    <div class="tile is-5 is-child box">
      <p class="title">Column Ib</p>
      <p> Cat ipsum dolor ...amet </p>
    </div>
      <div class="tile is-child box">
      <p class="title">Column Ic</p>
      <p> Cat ipsum dolor ...amet </p>
      </div>
  </div>
  <div class="tile is-parent">
    <div class="tile is-child box">
      <p class="title">Column II</p>
      <p>Lorem ipsum dolor sit...ut quam      </p>
      </div>
  </div>
</div>
```

In Listing 3-17, we initially create the main `<div>` element and assign it the ***tile is-ancestor*** class. Then we create the first child `<div>` element and assign it the ***tile is-parent*** and ***is-8*** classes to define it as a parent element and the 8-column size it occupies. Within this parent, we have created three `<div>` elements. We assign a title and sample text for each of them. But the only difference in the three `<div>` child elements of the parent is the size allocated to each of them. The first child is four columns long due to the *is-4* class. The second `<div>` child element is five columns long due to the *is-5* class. The third `<div>`, whose size is not defined, takes up the remaining space automatically. We also assign a box class to each child in conjunction with the size and child class to create a box container.

Then we create a separate `<div>` for the second parent of the ancestor tile. We assign the ***tile is-child*** and ***box*** classes to the child inside the second parent. We also define the title and sample content for this child.

The output of the code is shown in Figure 3-17.

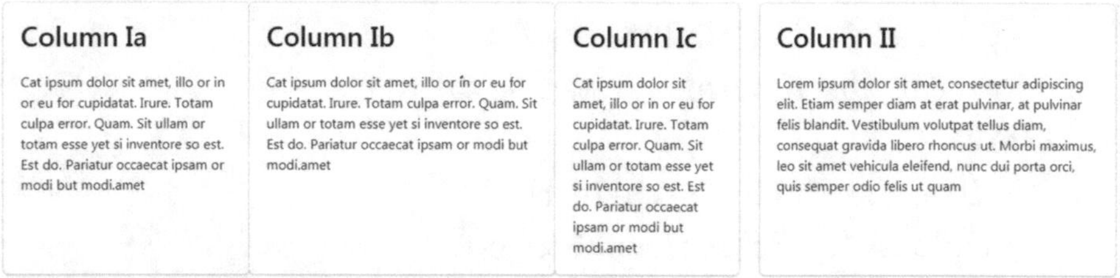

Figure 3-17. *Basic tile structure*

As you can see, the first parent occupies eight columns space and contains three child elements. The second parent has taken the remaining space of four columns automatically, as the size is not defined.

In Bulma, you can also stack tiles vertically. Let's understand it by using the example shown in Listing 3-18.

Listing 3-18. Stacking Tiles Vertically

```
<div class="tile is-ancestor">
  <div class="tile is-9 is-vertical notification is-parent">
    <div class="tile is-12 is-child notification is-danger box">
      <p class="title">Column Uno</p>
      <p> Cat ipsum dolor sit .... cupidatat </p>
    </div>
```

```
<div class="tile is-12 is-child notification is-primary box">
  <p class="title">Column Dos</p>
  <p> Cat ipsum dolor sit .... cupidatat </p>
</div>
  <div class="tile is-12 is-child notification is-info box">
  <p class="title">Column Tres</p>
  <p>Cat ipsum dolor sit .... cupidatat</p>
  </div>
</div>
<div class="tile notification is-success is-parent">
  <div class="tile is-child notification is-warning box">
    <p class="title">Column Four Lorem</p>
    <p>Lorem ipsum ... ut quam Column</p>
```

In Listing 3-18, we create one ancestor containing two parents. The first parent <div> is assigned a space of nine columns. We use the notification class to give it a bland contextual color. We also allocate the *is-vertical* class to this element. This will ensure that the child elements of the first parent tile will be stacked vertically. We create three child elements using *the is-child* class for each child <div> element.

For the first child element, we assign a tile of 12 columns of the parent size by using the *tile is-12* class, and we also use the *notification is-dange*r class to define the contextual color. Finally, we use the *box* class to create a box container for the first child. Thereon, we define the title and sample content for that child.

Similarly, we create two more child <div> elements. We assign the size of 12 columns for this child tile and define the *is-primary* and *is-info* classes to define its contextual colors. We also define a box container for their content using the *box* class, including the title and headings.

Following this, we create the second parent of the ancestor and define the contextual success color to the parent. Then we create a child for this parent and assign the contextual warning color to it. Moving forward, we define the title and sample content for this child.

The output of this code is shown in Figure 3-18.

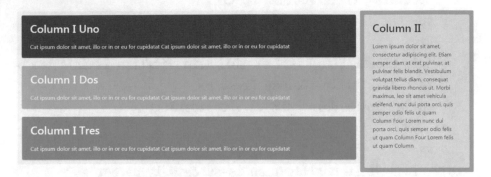

Figure 3-18. *Child tiles stacked vertically for first parent, and second parent-child defined normally*

As you can see, the first parent containing Column I Uno, Column I Dos, and Column I Tres child tiles are stacked vertically and occupy 12 columns horizontally. The second parent is a normal one with a single child. All parent columns and child columns show the size as defined in the code.

As explained earlier, you can have child elements much deeper within various parents. Let's see a code example.

Listing 3-19. Nested Child Element Under Various Parent Tiles

```
<div class="tile is-ancestor">
  <div class="tile is-8 is-vertical is-parent notification is-
  danger">
    <div class="tile is-12 is-child notification is-primary box">
      <p class="title is-size-4"><b>Column I Uno </b></p>
      <p>Cat ipsum dolor... cupidatat</p>
    </div>
    <div class="tile is-12 is-child box">
      <div class="tile is-parent">
      <div class="tile is-6 is-child notification is-warning
      box">
```

```
<p class="title is-size-4"><b>Column I Dos Sub-Child I
</b>  </p>
<p> Cat ipsum dolor... cupidatat </p>
</div>
<div class="tile is-child notification is-info box">
<p class="title is-size-4"><b>Column I Dos Sub-Child II
</b></p>
<p> Cat ipsum dolor... cupidatat </p>
</div>
</div>
</div>
</div>
<hr>
<div class="tile notification is-parent">
  <div class="tile is-child notification is-success box">
    <p class="title"><b>Column II </b></p>
    <p>Lorem ipsum dolor... orci,  </p>
  </div>
</div>
</div>
```

In Listing 3-19, we create a main <div> with the ***tile is-ancestor*** class. Then we create the first parent element and give it a size of eight columns with the ***is-vertical*** class so that its child elements are stacked. We give it a danger contextual notification color.

Then we create a 12-column child element under the first parent element and assign the primary contextual color to it. We create another 12-column element child element under the first parent. Under the second child element, we create a parent element and create a nested tile that is six columns wide, and a second child element that will occupy the remaining space with the info primary color.

Now we have designed the first parent tile and its child tiles, followed by a nested parent inside the second child element, which in turn contains two child tiles.

So, at the start of the code we used the ancestor tile. Under the ancestor child tile, we create the second parent tile and use the notification color for the second parent and assign the success contextual notification color to it. Then we define the title, subtitle, and sample content inside it.

The output of the complete code is shown in Figure 3-19:

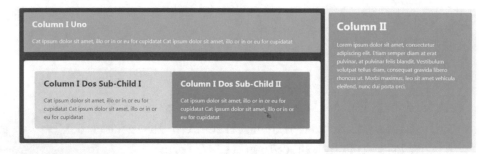

Figure 3-19. *Parent child, child tile, and nested child tiles*

Callout Panels and Box

Callout panels are containers with padding that create an inset box effect and highlight the content that separates it from the other usual content on a traditional web page. Apart from panels, Bulma also has a simple box element. Whereas boxes are used for normal content, panels are used for multiple elements like information sets and data tables, and may occasionally include forms. From a web design perspective, panels and boxes do not incorporate media and graphic content like cards or tiles do.

An important use of callout panels, in modern layouts especially, is to make the call-to-action elements stand out among the different content blocks. By singling out important information by adding more emphasis to a section or content, panels help get effective responses from the users.

We will see a step-by-step example of callout panels in Bulma in Listing 3-20.

Listing 3-20. Creating the First Panel

```
<div class="columns is-multiline">
  <div class="column is-5">
 <nav class="panel">
  <p class="panel-heading">
   <b> Brands </b></p>

  <p class="panel-tabs">
    <a class="is-active">All</a>
    <a>New</a>
    <a>Refurbished</a>
  </p>
  <a class="panel-block is-active">Samsung </a>
  <a class="panel-block"> Nokia </a>
  <a class="panel-block"> OnePlus </a>
  <a class="panel-block"> Honor </a>
  <a class="panel-block"> Redmi </a>
  <a class="panel-block"> Huawei </a>
  <a class="panel-block"> Motorola </a>
  <a class="panel-block"> Sony </a>
  <a class="panel-block"> Apple </a>
   <a class="panel-block"> Asus </a>
  </nav>
  </div>
 </div>
```

In Listing 3-20, we create the panel heading. Initially, we create a main <div> element and assign the *is-multiline* class to it in conjunction with the columns class. The entire code for the panels will be contained in the main <div> element.

79

Then, we define the column and assign a five-column width to it. Then we create the <nav> navigation element and assign the *panel* class to it. We move ahead to create a paragraph <p> element and assign the *panel-heading* class to it. We assign the **Brands** name as the panel heading. Then we create the panel tabs by using the *panel-tabs* class. Then we assign the names (All, New, and Refurbished) for the panel tabs. We add an *is-active* to the first panel tab, All.

Once the panel tabs are created, we create the list items using the <a> link tabs. For each link, we assign the *panel-block* class. We use the *is-active* class only for the first link, so that it shows that link chosen by default. Then we name different brand names of mobiles such as Samsung, Nokia, and Honor, to name a few.

The output of the code is shown in Figure 3-20.

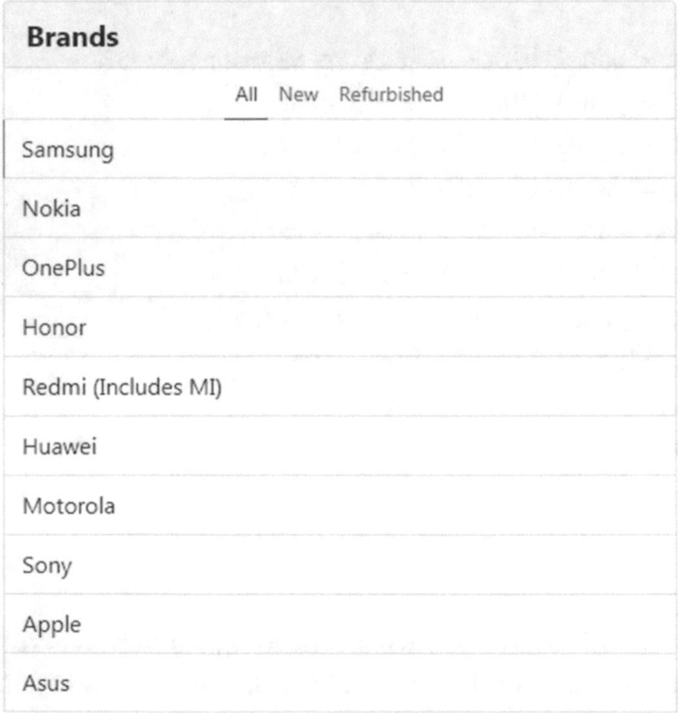

Brands
All   New   Refurbished
Samsung
Nokia
OnePlus
Honor
Redmi (Includes MI)
Huawei
Motorola
Sony
Apple
Asus

Figure 3-20. *Panel with mobile phone brands*

In Figure 3-20, we can see that the panel heading, panel tabs, and panel items are arranged as defined in the code. Then we define the second panel in the 12-column grid, which is assigned a size of 2 columns. We also use the *is-offset-1* class so that this panel is one column away from the first panel. Let's see the entire code for the second panel in Listing 3-21.

Listing 3-21. Creating the Second Panel

```
<div class="column is-2 is-offset-1">
  <nav class="panel">
  <p class="panel-heading">
    <b>Price</b>
  </p>
  <a class="panel-block">
  <= $100
  </a><a class="panel-block">
  <= $300
  </a><a class="panel-block">
  <= $500
  </a>
  <a class="panel-block">
  <= $750
    </a>
  </nav>
</div>
```

In Listing 3-21, we use the <nav> tag and assign the *panel* class to it. We define the panel-heading as Price, followed by the links containing the price rate range.

The output of this code is shown in Figure 3-21.

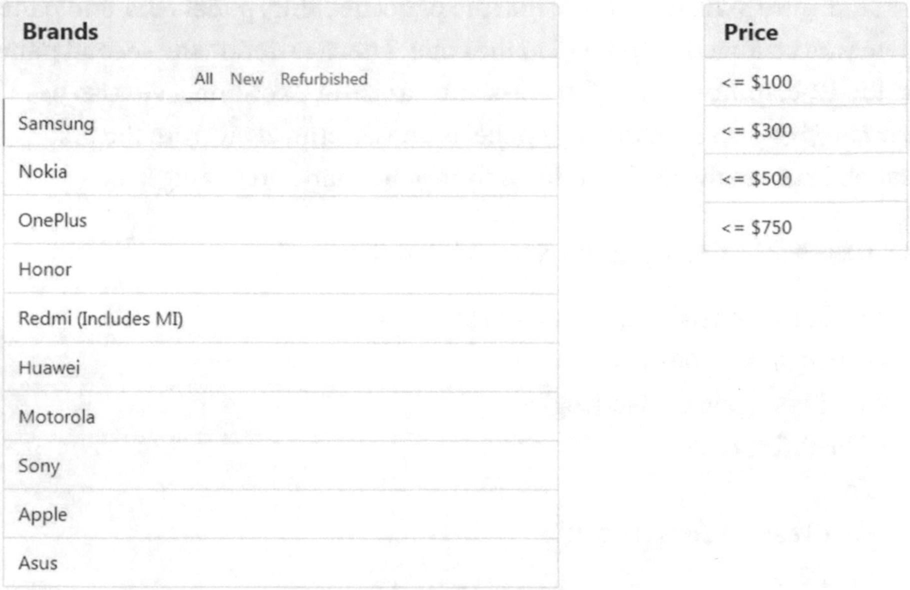

Brands				Price
	All New Refurbished			<= $100
Samsung				<= $300
Nokia				<= $500
OnePlus				<= $750
Honor				
Redmi (Includes MI)				
Huawei				
Motorola				
Sony				
Apple				
Asus				

Figure 3-21. *Second price range panel next to the first panel*

We then create another panel right below the second Price range panel.

Listing 3-22. Creating the Third Panel Below the Second Panel

```
<nav class="panel">
  <p class="panel-heading">
    <b>Color</b>
  </p>
  <p class="panel-block">
  <a class="button is-danger is-small"></a>
  </p>
  <p class="panel-block">
    <a class="button is-info is-small"></a>
  </p>
```

```
<p class="panel-block">
 <a class="button is-warning is-small"></a>
</p>
<p class="panel-block">
 <a class="button has-background-black is-small"></a>
</p>
<p class="panel-block">
 <a class="button has-background-gray-light is-small"></a>
</p>
</nav>
```

In the preceding code, we use a navigation <nav> element and then define the panel heading as Color. We create five color contextual buttons panel blocks using the <a> link with the **panel-block** class.

The output of the code so far is shown in Figure 3-22.

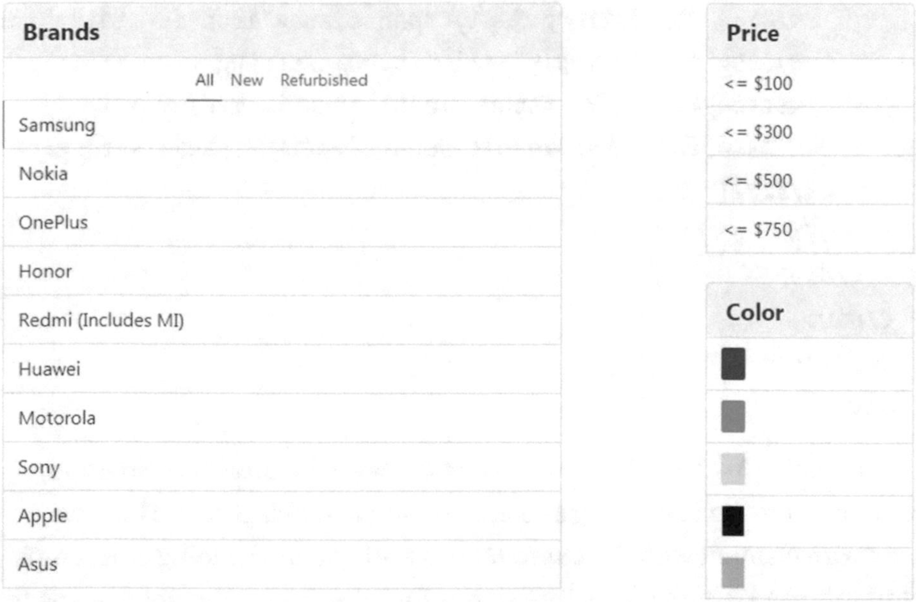

Brands			Price
	All New Refurbished		<= $100
Samsung			<= $300
Nokia			<= $500
OnePlus			<= $750
Honor			
Redmi (Includes MI)			Color
Huawei			■
Motorola			■
Sony			■
Apple			■
Asus			■

Figure 3-22. *Three panels for brands, price, and color*

Bulma also has a box layout, which we used previously in code. Let's see an example of the box container in Listing 3-23.

Listing 3-23. Defining the Box Container

```
<div class="box">
  <article class="media">
  <div class="media-content">
    <div class="content">
      <p>
        <strong class="is-size-4">Shrek-in-Matrix </strong>
        <br>
         Havana brown. Malkin. ..kittenz
        <br>
        <small><a><strong>Like <span class="icon is-medium"><i
        class="fas fa-heart"></i></span></strong>
        </a>   <a> <strong>Reply<span class="icon is-medium"><i
        class="fas fa-reply"></i></span></strong></a> ········
        <strong><a>Share <span class="icon is-medium"><i
        class="fas fa-share-alt-square"></i></span></strong><a>
        </small>
      </p>
    </div>
  </div>
  </article>
</div>
```

In Listing 3-23, we define a <div> class with the *box* class. Thereon, we define the <article> tag and assign the *media* class to it. Then, we create an element with the *content* class and add the heading and sample content in it. We also create three icons for Like, Reply, and Share using the Font Awesome-supported icon elements.

The output of the code is shown in Figure 3-23:

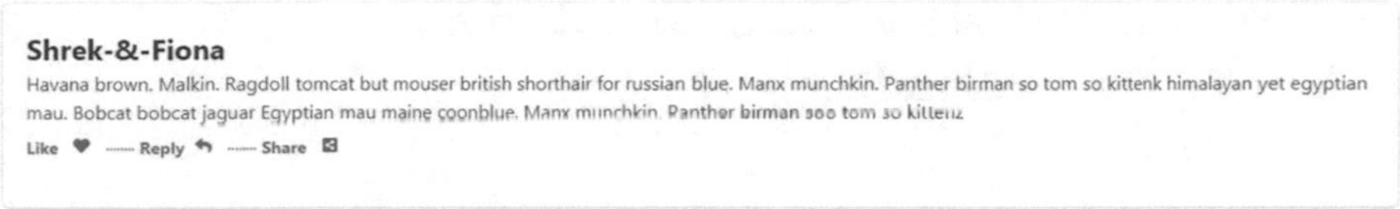

Shrek-&-Fiona

Havana brown. Malkin. Ragdoll tomcat but mouser british shorthair for russian blue. Manx munchkin. Panther birman so tom so kittenk himalayan yet egyptian mau. Bobcat bobcat jaguar Egyptian mau maine coonblue. Manx munchkin. Panther birman soo tom so kittenz

Like ♥ ── Reply ↰ ── Share ✉

Figure 3-23. *Box layout container*

Incorporating Footers

Footers help designers add common information and navigation options at the bottom of the web pages. Copyright information, sitemaps, privacy policies, and contact information are usually included in the footer section. Links to important pages of the web site are normally a part of the footer section (more so in single-page web site design). Streamlining the footer information is also a way to enhance the SEO and UX/UI aspects of your web site (think *good usability and readability practices*), specifically on mobile and tablet devices.

Let's see an example of a `<footer>` element in the following code (Listing 3-24). The Hero banner was explained earlier in the chapter; you may refer to that in Listing 3-12, which does not include the Hero footer part but does have sample content for the banner headings and body section. Only the footer section is explained here.

Listing 3-24. Creating Footer Design

```
<footer style="background-color: Aqua;">
  <br>
      <div  class="has-text-centered has-text-black">
          <b> © 1999-2007 Shrek-in-the-Matrix @All Rights
          Reserved</b>
          <br>
          <p>Cat ipsum dolor ...for cupidatat </p>
      <div><br>
```

```
<nav class="tabs is-boxed is-fullwidth">
<div class="container">
  <ul>
     <li>
     <a class="socicon-sharethis" style="border:2px
     solid White;"></a>
   </li>
   <li>
     <a class="socicon-facebook" style="border:2px solid
     White;"></a>
   </li>
   <li>
     <a class="socicon-twitter" style="border:2px solid
     White;"></a>
   </li>
   <li>
     <a class="socicon-snapchat" style="border:2px solid
     White;"></a>
   </li>
   <li>
     <a class="socicon-pinterest" style="border:2px
     solid White;"></a>
   </li>
   <li>
     <a class="socicon-linkedin" style="border:2px solid
     White;"></a>
   </li>
   <li>
     <a class="socicon-youtube" style="border:2px solid
     White;"></a>
   </li>
```

```
<li>
  <a class="socicon-whatsapp" style="border:2px solid
  White;"></a>
</li>
<li>
  <a class="socicon-tumblr" style="border:2px solid
  White;"></a>
</li>
<li>
  <a class="socicon-mail" style="border:2px solid
  White;"></a>
</li>
      </ul>
    </div>
  </nav>
</footer>
```

We use the `<footer>` element and assign the *Aqua* color to it. We enter the copyright sample message in the enclosed <p> tags. Then, we proceed to use a navigation <nav> element and assign the ***tabs***, ***is-boxed***, and ***is-fullwidth*** classes to it. Within that, we define a Bulma container using the ***container*** class. Similar to the Hero code, we create an unordered list of social media links from the Socicon web site.

The output of the code is shown in Figure 3-24.

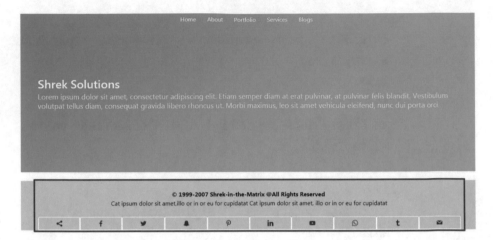

Figure 3-24. *Footer section highlighted in a red box*

Summary

In this chapter, we explored the different types of layout helpers such as containers, boxes, panels, media objects, and Hero banners, among others. These containers can be an alternative for grid structures, depending on the web site requirements.

In the next chapter, we will look at navigation and media components. These UI components are quite useful in building interactive web sites, a best fit for today's effective digital layouts.

CHAPTER 4

Navigation and Media Components

This chapter examines Bulma's navigation and media components. Bulma's intuitive and easy-to-use navigation components enable access to content and commercial functionalities such as checkout areas, while the media attributes enable sophisticated web design. Bulma's navigation components enable users to find content quickly and easily. They also help organize content in a streamlined manner, kind of a hallmark for efficient web design. Let's take a look at the various navigation and media elements.

Navigation Components

Navigation elements are an imperative aspect in designing modern layouts. They are used as a roadmap for the content on your site interface. Aesthetics account for nothing if your users cannot interact with your site easily. Therefore, navigation elements help visitors access that information quickly, eliminating the guesswork of finding the solution/content, which encouraged them to explore your web site in the first place. On a pan-optic level, navigation elements increase the user–site engagement and conversion rate while reducing the bounce rate significantly.

© Aravind Shenoy 2020
A. Shenoy, *Learning Bulma*, https://doi.org/10.1007/978-1-4842-5482-0_4

Bulma has several navigation components that streamline the usability factor significantly in a minimalistic way, without the bulk or clutter.

Bulma's navigation elements comprise breadcrumbs, drop-down menus, navbar (think *navigation bar*), and tabs that enable rapid user accessibility in a "no-frills" way.

Breadcrumbs

Breadcrumbs are a type of navigation system, which pinpoint the user location on the web app or web site. Breadcrumbs also improve site accessibility and exploration immensely, since they show the user location. The user can understand the hierarchy, and thus this navigation element is quite handy when there is massive content in the site.

Breadcrumbs are a common feature in web apps or sites that have several categories of displayed products/goods—this makes it easier to navigate to a particular category in case you want to check out the different products of similar make/genre. With an ultimate focus on site hierarchy, it enhances the way in which users are aware of the web page or any specific content location, paving the way for an excellent user experience.

Listing 4-1 explains the basic code for breadcrumbs.

Listing 4-1. Basic Breadcrumb Code

```
<div class="box">
 <nav class="breadcrumb" aria-label="breadcrumbs">
  <ul>
     <li class="is-active"><a href="#">Home</a></li>
     <li><a href="#">Documentation</a></li>
     <li><a href="#">Downloads</a></li>
     <li><a href="#">Support</a></li>
```

```
    <li><a href="#">Blogs</a></li>
    <li><a href="#" aria-current="page">Gallery</a></li>
    <li><a href="#">Contact</a></li>
  </ul>
 </nav>
</div>
```

In Listing 4-1, we create a box container by using the ***box*** class with a <div> element. Then we add a navigation element with the <nav> tag. We go on to assign the ***breadcrumb*** class to the <nav> tag. We create an unordered list using the parent <ul> and its child <li> tags.

To the first <li> tag, we assign the ***is-active*** class and name it Home. The ***is-active*** class will indicate the first <li> tag as the current active item. We then create six more <li> tags and name them accordingly, as seen in Listing 4-1.

The output of the code is shown in Figure 4-1.

Home / Documentation / Downloads / Support / Blogs / Gallery / Contact

Figure 4-1. *Basic breadcrumb*

In the Bulma breadcrumb component, you can align the breadcrumb to the right or center. Bulma supports different separators like bullet separator, has-succeeds separator, and the arrow separator.

In Listing 4-2, we align the breadcrumb to the right and change the separator to an arrow separator.

Listing 4-2. Right-Align Breadcrumb with Arrow Separator

```
<div class="container">
 <nav class="breadcrumb has-arrow-separator is-right" aria-
label="breadcrumbs">
  <ul>
     <li class="is-active"><a href="#">Home</a></li>
     <li><a href="#">Documentation</a></li>
     <li><a href="#">Downloads</a></li>
     <li><a href="#">Support</a></li>
     <li><a href="#">Blogs</a></li>
     <li><a href="#" aria-current="page">Gallery</a></li>
     <li><a href="#">Contact</a></li>
  </ul>
</nav>
```

As you see, most of the code is the same as in Listing 4-1. Instead of the box layout, we use the ***container*** class as the main <div> element instead of a box layout.

Coming back to the relevant stuff, we add the classes ***has-arrow-separator*** and ***is-right*** alongside the default ***breadcrumb*** class in the <nag> tag. The rest of the code is the same, where we create an unordered list and define the name for each list item.

The output of the code is shown in Figure 4-2.

Home → Documentation → Downloads → Support → Blogs → Gallery → Contact

Figure 4-2. *Right-aligned breadcrumb with an arrow separator*

Moving forward, in Listing 4-3 we have an example of breadcrumbs aligned to the center of the layout. Breadcrumbs in Bulma have small, medium, and large classes apart from the default normal class, using which you can change the size of the breadcrumb as in Listing 4-3.

Listing 4-3. Centered Breadcrumb with Different Sizes and Separators

```
<div class="container">
 <nav class="breadcrumb is-small is-centered has-bullet-
separator" aria-label="breadcrumbs">
  <ul>
     <li class="is-active"><a href="#">Home</a></li>
     <li><a href="#">Documentation</a></li>
     <li><a href="#">Downloads</a></li>
     <li><a href="#">Support</a></li>
     <li><a href="#">Blogs</a></li>
     <li><a href="#" aria-current="page">Gallery</a></li>
     <li><a href="#">Contact</a></li>
  </ul>
</nav>
</div>
<br><br><br>
<div class="container">
<nav class="breadcrumb is-large is-centered has-succeeds-
separator" aria-label="breadcrumbs">
  <ul>
     <li class="is-active"><a href="#">Home</a></li>
     <li><a href="#">Documentation</a></li>
     <li><a href="#">Downloads</a></li>
     <li><a href="#">Support</a></li>
     <li><a href="#">Blogs</a></li>
     <li><a href="#" aria-current="page">Gallery</a></li>
     <li><a href="#">Contact</a></li>
  </ul>
 </nav>
</div>
```

In Listing 4-3, we create a container for the first breadcrumb. We use the *is-small* class, *is-centered*, and *has-bullet-separator* in conjunction with the *breadcrumb* class for the first breadcrumb. The rest of the code for the first breadcrumb is similar to the earlier code listings, where we create an unordered list to define names for the breadcrumbs.

Then we create the second breadcrumb inside another container where we add the *is-large* class, *is-centered*, and *has-succeeds-separator* classes in conjunction with the *breadcrumb* class. The rest of the code is the same as earlier examples, where we create an unordered list and define the names of the breadcrumb items.

The output of the code is shown in Figure 4-3.

Home · Documentation · Downloads · Support · Blogs · Gallery · Contact

Home > Documentation > Downloads > Support > Blogs > Gallery > Contact

Figure 4-3. *Centered breadcrumbs in small and large sizes*

As you can see in Figure 4-3, both the breadcrumbs are aligned to the center. While the first breadcrumb is small in size, the breadcrumb below is large in size. Observe the bullet separator and has-succeeds separators for the first and last breadcrumbs, respectively.

You can also use icons in conjunction with the breadcrumb items. Listing 4-4 shows an example of merging icons with the breadcrumbs in Bulma.

Listing 4-4. Merging Icons with Breadcrumbs

```
<div class="container">
 <nav class="breadcrumb is-centered" aria-label="breadcrumbs">
  <ul>
    <li>
      <a>
```

```
    <span class="icon is-small"><i class="fas fa-home"></
    i> </span>
      <span>Home</span>
    </a>
</li>
<li>
  <a>
      <span class="icon is-small"><i class="fas fa-
      download"></i> </span>
      <span>Downloads</span>
  </a>
</li>
<li>
  <a>
      <span class="icon is-small"><i class="fas fa-file-
      contract"></i> </span>
      <span>Products</span>
  </a>

</li>
<li class="is-active">
  <a>
      <span class="icon is-small"><i class="fas fa-users-
      cog"></i> </span>
      <span>Support</span>
  </a>
</li>
<li>
  <a>
      <span class="icon is-small"><i class="fab fa-
      dochub"></i> </span>
      <span>Docs</span>
```

```
        </a>
      </li>
      <li>
        <a>
            <span class="icon is-small"><i class="fab fa-
            blogger-b"></i> </span>
            <span>Blogs</span>
        </a>
      </li>
      <li>
        <a>
            <span class="icon is-small"><i class="fas fa-phone-
            alt"></i> </span>
            <span>Contact</span>
        </a>
      </li>
    </ul>
  </nav>
</div>
```

In Listing 4-4, we define a main <div> with the ***container*** class. Inside
we create another <div> element and assign the ***breadcrumb*** class in
conjunction with the ***is-centered*** class to position the breadcrumb at the
center of the row.

Then we create the breadcrumb using the unordered lists with the <ul>
and <li> tags. The only difference is that we use the <span> element within
each <li> class and define an icon next to the breadcrumb item name. For
example, within the <a> tags within the first <li> tag, we define a Home
icon within the span tags using the following line of code.

```
<span class="icon is-small"><i class="fas fa-home"></i> </
span>
```

* * creates an empty space after the icon. We have also used the *is-small* class in the span tag and the home icon within the <i> tags, which are within the <span> tags.

We have used the latest Font Awesome 5.x icons. For that, we have used the following link in the <head> section before the <body> section of the code:

```
<link rel="stylesheet" href="https://cdnjs.cloudflare.
com/ajax/libs/font-awesome/5.10.2/css/all.min.css"
integrity="sha256-zmfNZmXoNWBMemUOo1XUGFfcOihGGLYdgtJS3KCr/lo="
crossorigin="anonymous" />
```

Then, we define different icons within each <li> tag for each breadcrumb item based on the relevant names. Also, we have kept the Support breadcrumb item as the current item using the *is-active* class.

The output of the code is shown in Figure 4-4.

🏠 Home / ⬇ Downloads / 📄 Products / 👥 Support / Ɗ Docs / ✉ Blogs 📞 Contact

Figure 4-4. Breadcrumb with icons

Drop-Downs

Drop-downs are usually created to show the different items/content in a compact way—for example, the distinct categories commonly seen on e-commerce web sites are designed in a panel-like drop-down. You can design an apt site structure and include diverse menu items in a drop-down, eliminating too many links or congestion on the web page. Apart from a clean layout, it also eliminates the need to scroll repeatedly, as the user can access specific information from the links in the drop-down list.

From a UX/UI perspective, you have to consider the mobile platform, where it becomes a different ballgame altogether due to the touch feature and highly compact screens. Also, the links, data, or information in a drop-down should be well organized in line with the user needs. Bulma's drop-down feature is tailored for all platforms, and is especially compatible with the mobile screen interface owing to its mobile-first paradigm.

Let's see the process of creating drop-down menus in Bulma (Listing 4-5).

Listing 4-5. Creating a Drop-Down Menu

```
<div class="dropdown is-active">
  <div class="dropdown-trigger">
    <button class="button has-background-white-bis">
      <span>Services</span>
      <span class="icon is-small">
        <i class="fas fa-angle-down" aria-hidden="true"></i>
      </span>
    </button>
  </div>
  <div class="dropdown-menu" id="dropdown-menu" role="menu">
    <div class="dropdown-content">
      <a href="#" class="dropdown-item item is-active">
        Web Design
      </a>
      <a class="dropdown-item">
        Mobile app Development
      </a>
      <a href="#" class="dropdown-item">
        SEO
      </a>
      <a href="#" class="dropdown-item">

      </a>
      <a href="#" class="dropdown-item">
        PPC
      </a>
```

```
  <hr class="dropdown-divider">
  <a href="#" class="dropdown-item">
    UX/UI design
  </a>
  <a href="#" class="dropdown-item">
    Email Marketing Creative Design
  </a>
  <a href="#" class="dropdown-item">
     Logo & Brand Identity Design
  </a>
 </div>
 </div>
</div>
```

In Listing 4-5, we create a <div> element with the ***dropdown*** class to make it a main container. For the drop-down button, we create another <div> element and assign the ***dropdown-trigger*** class to it. Within this <div>, we define the drop-down button with a white background and, using the icon in conjunction with the button element, we create a small drop-down arrow.

Once we are done with the drop-down button, we create a separate drop-down menu where we will define the drop-down content. We create a <div> and assign the ***dropdown-menu*** class to it. Within that <div>, we create a child <div> and assign the ***dropdown-content*** to it. Next, we create several links using the anchor <a> link tags with the ***dropdown-item*** classes.

After we define four links, we create a drop-down divider using the <hr> tags with the ***dropdown-divider*** class. Thereon, we create three more links using the <a> tags with the ***dropdown-item*** class for each link.

The output of the code is shown in Figure 4-5.

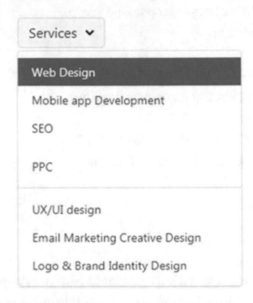

Figure 4-5. *Drop-down menu*

You can also use prose content instead of links in the drop-down content. For that, use <div> for each drop-down item instead of the <a> link tags. You can also use a hover effect, which will display the drop-down menu items on hover.

Listing 4-6. Using Content for Drop-Downs with Hover Facility

```
<div class="dropdown is-hoverable">
  <div class="dropdown-trigger">
    <button class="button has-background-white-ter">
      <span>Services</span>
      <span class="icon is-small">
        <i class="fas fa-angle-down" aria-hidden="true"></i>
      </span>
    </button>
  </div>
```

```
<div class="dropdown-menu" id="dropdown-menu" role="menu">
  <div class="dropdown-content">

     <div href="#" class="dropdown-item">
      Cat ipsum dolor sit amet, molestiae deserunt. Quam lorem
      aut. Ipsa magnam yet quo
     </div>
     <hr class="dropdown-divider">
     <div href="#" class="dropdown-item">
      Adipisci sit but omnis quae. Aute eius for
      exercitationem occaecat commodi so abb
     </div>
       <hr class="dropdown-divider">
        <div href="#" class="dropdown-item">
      sit amet, molestiae deserunt. Quam lorem aut. Ipsa
      magnam yet quo aut. Ipsa magnam
       </div>
    </div>
  </div>
</div>
</div>
```

In Listing 4-6, we create similar drop-down functionality but we add the *is-hoverable* class in conjunction with the *dropdown* class for the main <div> element. Then, we create the drop-down button as in the earlier example.

The difference is when we create the drop-down menu. Within the <div> with the *dropdown-content* class, we create <div> elements and assign the *dropdown-item* class to each of the menu items as shown in Listing 4-6.

The output of the code will display a drop-down button called Services and, on hovering over it, you can see the drop-down menu items as shown in Figure 4-6.

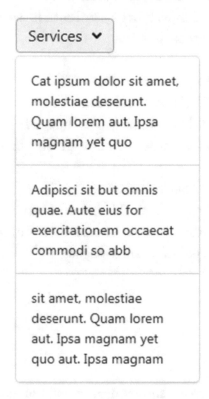

Figure 4-6. *Drop-down menu with prose content on hover action*

Tabs

Tabs are an excellent navigation system due to the linear representation of the site structure. Tabs not only help you divide the content into separate sections but also provide a way to access that content. Their intuitive architecture makes users aware of their location on the site quickly.

However, the usability factor of the navigation tabs element depends on how you organize and use their functionality—for example, the heading for each tab should have minimal characters or shorter lengths. Tabs are quite effective when you want to show a string of similar categories/similar genres.

Bulma's tabs component is quite easy to design and helps site/app's visitors to access chunks of data in a simple way. However, web designers/developers should take into account the specific user needs, amount of data, and how rapidly users can access that content.

Let's look at the procedure to create tabs in Bulma, as seen in Listing 4-7.

Listing 4-7. Creating Basic Tabs

```
<div class="tabs">
  <ul>
    <li class="is-active"><a>Home</a></li>
    <li><a>About</a></li>
    <li><a>Downloads</a></li>
    <li><a>Support</a></li>
    <li><a>Gallery</a></li>
    <li><a>Tutorials</a></li>
    <li><a>Documentation</a></li>
    <li><a>Contact</a></li>
  </ul>
</div>
```

In Listing 4-7, we create a main <div> element and assign the ***tabs*** class to it. Then we create an unordered list within that <div> using the <ul> and <li> tags. We assign the ***is-active*** class to the first <li> tag to make it the current item.

The output of the code is shown in Figure 4-7.

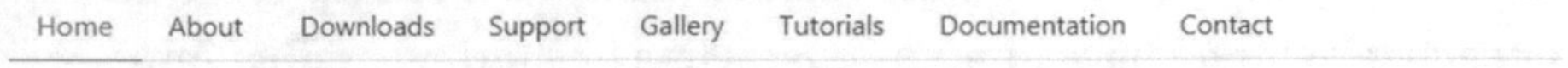

Home   About   Downloads   Support   Gallery   Tutorials   Documentation   Contact

Figure 4-7. *Tabs navigation system*

As you can see, we have a simple navigation system.

You can also align the tabs at the center or right and change the size to small, large, or medium using the respective classes. You can use icons for each tab in tandem with the name. Apart from that, you can create a classic tabs look using the boxed functionality, as shown in Listing 4-8.

Listing 4-8. Defining Classic-Style Tabs with Boxed Attribute

```
<div class="tabs is-centered is-large is-boxed">
  <ul>
    <li class="is-active">
      <a>
        <span class="icon is-small"><i class="fas fa-home"></
        i> </span>
         <span>Home</span>
      </a>
    </li>

    <li>
      <a>
          <span class="icon is-small"><i class="fas fa-
          download"></i> </span>
          <span>Downloads</span>
      </a>
    </li>
    <li>
      <a>
```

```
      <span class="icon is-small"><i class="fas fa-file-
      contract"></i> </span>
      <span>Products</span>
   </a>
</li>

<li>
   <a>
      <span class="icon is-small"><i class="fas fa-users-
      cog"></i> </span>
      <span>Support</span>
   </a>
</li>

<li>
   <a>
      <span class="icon is-small"><i class="fab fa-
      dochub"></i> </span>
      <span>Docs</span>
   </a>
</li>
<li>
   <a>
      <span class="icon is-small"><i class="fab fa-
      blogger-b"></i> </span>
      <span>Blogs</span>
   </a>
</li>

   <a>
      <span class="icon is-small"><i class="fas fa-phone-
      alt"></i> </span>
      <span>Contact</span>
```

```
      </a>
    </li>

  </ul>
</div>
```

In Listing 4-8, we create the parent <div> and assign the **tabs** class to it
as seen in the earlier example. In conjunction with the tabs class, we also
use the following classes:

- **is-centered** class for aligning tabs to the center

- **is-large** class for creating large-sized tabs

- **is-boxed** class for the classic tabs look

Within the parent <div>, we create an unordered list using the <ul>
and <li> tags. We use the <span> tags within link <a> tags for each <li> tags
as shown in the following line of code:

```
<span class="icon is-small"><i class="fas fa-home"></i> </
span> <span>Home</span>
```

Similarly, we create several tabs items.

The output of the code is shown in Figure 4-8.

Figure 4-8. *Boxed tabs with icons at the center*

As you can see from the output, the tabs are positioned at the center of
the row and have the relevant items next to the tab names. Moreover, you
can also see the classic boxed look for the Home tab, which is the default
current tab as defined in the code.

You can also define an exclusive look to each tab, where each tab will
have a border. This is done with the toggle class. You can also use rounded
borders for the first and last tabs, as shown in Listing 4-9.

Listing 4-9. Rounded Shape Tabs with Exclusive Borders

```
<div class="tabs is-boxed is-toggle is-toggle-rounded">
 <ul>
   <li class="is-active">
     <a>
       <span class="icon is-small"><i class="fas fa-home"></
       i> </span>
       <span>Home</span>
     </a>
   </li>

   <li>
     <a>
       <span class="icon is-small"><i class="fas fa-
       download"></i> </span>
       <span>Downloads</span>
     </a>
   </li>
   <li>
     <a>
       <span class="icon is-small"><i class="fas fa-file-
       contract"></i> </span>
       <span>Products</span>
     </a>
   </li>

   <li>
     <a>
       <span class="icon is-small"><i class="fas fa-users-
       cog"></i> </span>
       <span>Support</span>
     </a>
```

```
      </li>
<li>
    <a>
        <span class="icon is-small"><i class="fab fa-
        dochub"></i> </span>
        <span>Docs</span>
    </a>
  </li>
  <li>
    <a>
        <span class="icon is-small"><i class="fab fa-
        blogger-b"></i> </span>
        <span>Blogs</span>
    </a>
  </li>
  <li>
    <a>
        <span class="icon is-small"><i class="fas fa-
        images"></i> </span>
        <span>Gallery</span>
    </a>
  </li>
  <li>
    <a>
        <span class="icon is-small"><i class="fas fa-phone-
        alt"></i> </span>
        <span>Contact</span>
    </a>
  </li>
 </ul>
</div>
```

In Listing 4-9, we use the ***is-boxed*** and ***is-toggle*** classes together in conjunction with the ***tabs*** class to allocate a boxed border for each tab. We also use another class, ***is-toggle-rounded***, in conjunction with those classes to give a rounded border for the first and last tabs.

The rest of the code is similar to the earlier example, where we have created tabs with icons using an unordered list.

The output of the code is shown in Figure 4-9.

Figure 4-9. *Boxed border for all tabs with rounded borders at each end*

Navbar

Bulma's navbar element helps design a horizontal list of links enabling site visitors to access any section in the site. However, from a UI/UX perspective, it has to be minimalistic and simple. The headings should be short in length and the number of headings should be not more than 5 or 6, as it may create unnecessary clutter. You should never design a navbar first and then fit in the content. In fact, it should be the other way around—the navbar should be designed keeping content at the crux of your site structure, to ensure high-degree of readability and rapid access.

Let's examine the navbar design in Bulma, as shown in Listing 4-10.

Listing 4-10. Creating a Simple Navbar

```
<nav class="navbar has-background-grey">
<div class="navbar-brand">
    <a class="navbar-item" href="https://pixabay.com/photos/
    oracle-girl-photomontage-witch-2133976/">
        <img src="Images/Oracle.png" alt="Oracle">
    </a>
```

```
        <a class="navbar-burger burger" data-target="navMenu">
          <span></span>
          <span></span>
          <span></span>
        </a>
</div>
<div id="navMenu" class="navbar-menu">
<div class="navbar-start">

          <a href="#" class="navbar-item has-text-white is-active">
          <b>Horoscope</b></a>
          <a href="#" class="navbar-item has-text-white">
          <b>Astrology</b></a>
          <a href="#" class="navbar-item has-text-white">
          <b>Psychics Experts</b></a>
          <a href="#" class="navbar-item has-text-white">
          <b>Predictions</b></a>
          <a href="#" class="navbar-item has-text-white">
          <b>Occult</b></a>
   </strong>
        </div>

<div class="navbar-end">
        <div class="navbar-item">
          <div class="buttons">
            <a class="button is-outlined">
              <strong>Login</strong>
            </a>

        </div>
```

```
      </div>
    </div>

  </div>
</nav>
```

In Listing 4-10, we define a navigation element <nav> and assign the ***navbar*** class to it. The ***navbar*** class results in a navigation bar container. Within the <nav> tags, we create a main < div> tag and assign the ***navbar-brand*** class to it. This navbar-brand element is the left side of the navbar, which is always visible and usually contains logo and links. Thereon, we create an anchor tag and assign the ***navbar-item*** class to it. The ***navbar-item*** class usually is used for various items on the navbar, but here we use it for the anchor link, pointing toward a site. Then we define the logo using the <img> tag.

Next, we create the hamburger icon, which is called the ***navbar-burger*** in Bulma. For this, we create another anchor tag and assign the ***navbar-burger*** class to it. We use a ***burger*** class in conjunction with the ***navbar-burger*** class to facilitate action using JavaScript. We set a ***data-target*** attribute and assign the value ***Navicon*** to it. We create three <span> elements without any label or name for creating three lines of the hamburger icon functionality.

Once we are done with the navburger, we create a separate <div> and assign the ***navbar-menu*** class to it. We also assign an id, whose value is the ***Navicon***, which incidentally is also the value of the data-target attribute mentioned earlier.

Then we create another <div> tag within the preceding <div> and define the ***navbar-start*** class to it, which will align the navbar menu to the left of the logo. We move on to create five anchor links and assign the ***navbar-item*** class to each of them, and define the menu items on the navbar at the left of the logo.

Next, we create another <div> and assign the ***navbar-end*** class to it. This will align the menu-items defined here to the right of the navbar. We define a <div> element within it and assign the ***navbar-item*** class to it. We create a Login button and assign the ***is-outlined*** class to it.

The output of the code is shown in Figure 4-10.

Figure 4-10. *Navbar with logo and menu items*

Media Components

Media components help display media in different ways, depending on their use cases or functionality. In this section, we will look at progress bars, notifications, images, tags, and pagination components in Bulma.

Progress Bars

A progress bar is an excellent way of showing the progress of any action. It is usually an indicator of the downloading process and enables the user to visualize the progression of the download operation.

Bulma's progress bar is explained in Listing 4-11.

Listing 4-11. Creating Progress Bars with Contextual Colors

```
<div class="box">
<progress class="progress is-primary" value="15"
max="100">15%</progress>
<progress class="progress is-warning" value="35"
max="100">35%</progress>
</div>
```

In Listing 4-11, we create a box container and define two progress bars. We use the <progress> element and assign a *progress* class to it, and also assign a contextual primary color to it using the *is-primary* class. We set the bar value as 15, with 100 being the maximum value. For this, we use the *value* attribute and the *max* attribute.

Next, we similarly define the second progress bar with 35 as the value and a maximum value of 100. We assign the contextual warning color to it.

The output of the code is shown in Figure 4-11.

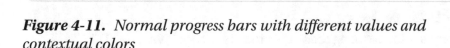

Figure 4-11. *Normal progress bars with different values and contextual colors*

In Bulma, you can assign different sizes to the progress bars. In Listing 4-12, we use the *is-medium* class for the progress bars with different contextual colors.

Listing 4-12. Creating Progress Bars with Medium Size

```
<div class="box">
<progress class="progress is-info is-medium" value="50"
max="100">50%</progress>
<progress class="progress is-success is-medium" value="65"
max="100">65%</progress>
</div>
```

In Listing 4-12, we create two progress bars and assign the values 50 and 65 in conjunction with the progress class. We use the *is-medium* size class for both progress bars. We also define the contextual colors by assigning the *is-info* and *is-success* classes to them, respectively.

113

The output of the code is shown in Figure 4-12.

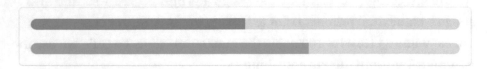

Figure 4-12. *Progress bars with medium-size and contextual colors*

Next, we see the effect of the large class, which results in large-sized progress bars, in Listing 4-13.

Listing 4-13. Creating Large-Sized Progress Bars

```
<div class="box">
<progress class="progress is-link is-large" value="77"
max="100">77%</progress>
<progress class="progress is-danger is-large" value="90"
max="100">90%</progress>
</div>
```

In Listing 4-13, we create two progress bars and assign the ***is-large*** class in conjunction with the ***progress*** class to each of them. We define the link and danger contextual colors to the two progress bars, and also define 77 and 90 as the values for the two progress bars.

The output of the code is shown in Figure 4-13.

Figure 4-13. *Large-sized progress bars with contextual colors*

If we do not assign any value to the progress bar, it will result in an intermediate buffering state for the progress bar, as shown in Listing 4-14.

Listing 4-14. Creating Intermediate Buffering State Progress Bars

```
<div class="box">
<progress class="progress is-primary" max="100">15%</progress>
<progress class="progress is-warning" max="100">35%</progress>
</div>
```

In Listing 4-14, we have created 2 progress bars with different contextual colors but we have not used a value attribute though we have retained the max attribute.

The output of the code is shown in Figure 4-14.

Figure 4-14. *Buffering progress bars without values*

Notifications

Notifications are a visual aid to attract the attention of the users. At times, they prompt the users to complete an action; sometimes they may be used to show important/helpful information to the users. Updates/alerts are types of notifications, while push subscription messages/context pop-ups are other use cases usually found in modern layouts.

Bulma's notification element is quite easy to code, as shown in Listing 4-15.

Listing 4-15. Creating Basic Notifications

```
<div class="columns is-multiline">
   <div class="column is-5 notification is-primary">
   <button class="delete"></button>
    cat ipsum dolor sit amet, eos...
   </div>
   <div class="column is-5 is-offset-1 notification is-link">
   <button class="delete"></button>
    cat ipsum dolor sit amet, eos...
   </div>

   <div class="column is-half is-offset-2 notification">
   <button class="delete"></button>
    cat ipsum dolor sit amet, eos...
   </div>
</div>
```

In Listing 4-15, we first create a columns container and assign the *is-multiline* class in conjunction with the columns class. Then we define three columns of different sizes. Inside each <div> element column, we use the ***notification*** class and also create a delete button for those notifications by using the ***delete*** class for each <button> element.

The first column occupies the space of five columns, whereas the second column is allocated a space of five columns and is offset by one column. The third column is assigned the space of half the 12-column grid and is assigned an offset of two columns. While the first notification is assigned a primary contextual color, the second notification is assigned the link contextual color using the ***is-primary*** and ***is-link*** classes, respectively. The third notification is not assigned any color and will take up the default color for the notification attribute.

The output of the code on a tablet screen is shown in Figure 4-15.

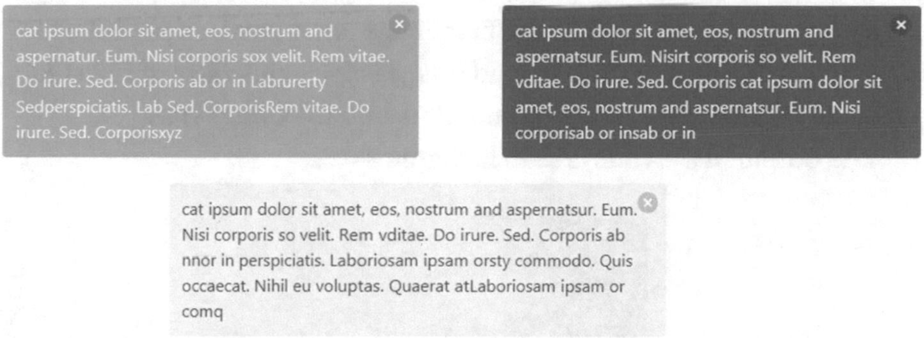

Figure 4-15. *Different colored notification columns with the delete button*

Images

Bulma's image element is a container for responsive images or pictures. Bulma's image element can not only be used for creating rounded and Retina images but also for defining ratio-based responsive images—for example, images used in still photography displayed consistently on various devices/screen-sizes.

To understand Bulma's image component, let's look at the Listing 4-16.

Listing 4-16. Creating Two Different Image Sizes for the Same Picture

```
<figure class="image is-48x48">
  <img src="Images/Shrek.png" alt="Shrek">
 </figure>
<br><br><br>
<figure class="image is-128x128">
  <img src="Images/Shrek.png" alt="Shrek">
</figure>
```

In Listing 4-16, we use two <figure> tags for the same image, with the *image* class assigned to each of them. We use the <img> tag for defining the source of the image. While the first image is assigned a size of 48×48 using the *is-48×48 class*, the second image is assigned a size of 128×128 using the *is-128×128* class in conjunction with the *image* class.

The output of the code is seen in Figure 4-16.

Figure 4-16. *Same image with different sizes*

You can add a rounded shape to the image, as shown in Listing 4-17.

Listing 4-17. Defining a Rounded Image Container

```
<figure class="image is-128x128">
  <img class="is-rounded" src="Images/Shrek.png" alt="Shrek">
</figure>
```

In Listing 4-17, we use the <figure> tag and assign a size of 128×128 to the image. Next, for the <img> tag, we assign the ***is-rounded*** class, which gives a rounded border shape to the image.

The output of the code is shown in Figure 4-17.

Figure 4-17. *Rounded border image*

If you do not know the exact dimensions, you can still define a ratio for the images.

Bulma has the following 16 ratio modifiers for the image element:

- ***image is-square***

- ***image is-1by1***

- ***image is-5by4***

- ***image is-4by3***

- ***image is-3by2***

- *image is-5by3*

- *image is-16by9*

- *image is-2by1*

- *image is-3by1*

- *image is-4by5*

- *image is-3by4*

- *image is-2by3*

- *image is-3by5*

- *image is-9by16*

- *image is-1by2*

- *image is-1by3*

Let's see an example of a ratio modifier using the image element in Listing 4-18.

Listing 4-18. Creating Ratio Modifier-Based Image Containers

```
<figure class="image is-3by2">
  <img src="Images/Fiona.png" alt="Fiona">
</figure>
```

In Listing 4-18, we use the <figure> tags and use the ***is-3by2*** ratio modifier class in conjunction with the image class. Then we define the image source using the <img> tag.

The output of the code is seen in Figure 4-18.

Figure 4-18. *Image ratio modifier (3by2)*

Tags

In blogs you may see tags, which are labels that are relevant to that article. It is a handy element in today's digital design era, especially used in digital photos programs, web pages, blogs, articles, and social media platforms.

A particular use case is in blogs where you promote your products/ goods. You will use relevant tags to increase the scope of the product. But your site visitors/users may come out with different tags, which may be market-based, location-based, or context-based. For example, consider a blog on a datacenter. You may use tags like "Data-Center operations," "Digital Datacenters," and "Innovation-in-Datacenters" for your company blog/article. Your users/customers/readers may add tags like "colocation," "digital transformation," "IoT," "DCIM," "Sustainability," "Data-center

Planning," and "Data-center-Energy-Efficiency" or even their company name to increase the reach and exposure of their solutions/concepts.

To understand how to use the tag component in Bulma, let's look at Listing 4-19.

Listing 4-19. Basic Tags with Different Contextual Colors

```
<div class="box">
<p class="has-text-centered">
<span class="tag is-primary">WhatsApp</span>
<span class="tag is-link">Facebook</span>
<span class="tag is-success">Share</span>
</p>
</div>
```

In Listing 4-19, we create a box container within which we define a paragraph tag <p> and assign the ***has-text-centered*** class to it so that the output is centered. Then we create three tags using the ***tag*** class. We enclose it in three <span> elements and after assigning the ***tag*** class to each <span> element, we assign different contextual colors—primary, link, and success—to the three <span> elements, respectively.

The output of the code is shown in Figure 4-19.

Figure 4-19. *Tags with different contextual colors*

You can also assign rounded borders to the tags by using is-rounded in conjunction with the tag class. For example, check out Listing 4-20.

Listing 4-20. Defining Rounded Tags

```
<div class="box">
<p class="has-text-centered">
<span class="tag is-rounded is-warning">Snapchat</span>
<span class="tag is-rounded is-danger">YouTube</span>
<span class="tag is-rounded is-info">Twitter</span>
</div>
```

The code in Listing 4-20 is almost the same as that in Listing 4-19, but it uses the *is-rounded* class in conjunction with the **tag** and contextual color classes.

The output of the code is shown in Figure 4-20.

Figure 4-20. *Rounded tags*

You can also use the medium and large classes to increase the size of the tags. Check out Listing 4-21.

Listing 4-21. Defining Different Sizes for the Tags

```
<div class="box">
<div>
<span class="tag is-success">Share</span>
<span class="tag is-warning">Snapchat</span>
</div>
<br><hr><br>
<div class="tags are-medium">
<span class="tag is-primary">WhatsApp</span>
<span class="tag is-link">Facebook</span>
</div>
```

```
<br><hr><br>
<div class="tags are-large">
<span class="tag is-danger">YouTube</span>
<span class="tag is-info">Twitter</span>
</div>
</div>
```

In Listing 4-21, we create a box container and define three <div> elements. Within the first <div> tags, we create two <span> elements, and assign the *tag* class with different contextual color classes.

Then we create another <div> and we assign the **tags *are-medium*** class to it.

Within this <div> tag, we create two <span> elements and assign the *tag* class in conjunction with the contextual color classes.

Moving forward, we create a third <div> element and assign the ***are-large*** class to it.

Then we similarly create two <span> elements and assign the contextual classes to them in conjunction with the *tag* class.

The output of the code is shown in Figure 4-21.

Figure 4-21. *Different sized tags*

You can also attach two tags together. Check out the code example in Listing 4-22.

Listing 4-22. Tag Addon Feature Combining Both Tags

```
<div class="box">
<div class="tags has-addons">
<span class="tag is-success">Share</span>
<span class="tag is-warning">Snapchat</span>
</div>
<br>
<div class="tags has-addons are-medium">
<span class="tag is-primary">WhatsApp</span>
<span class="tag is-link">Facebook</span>
</div>
<br>
<div class="tags has-addons are-large">
<span class="tag is-danger">YouTube</span>
<span class="tag is-info">Twitter</span>
</div>
</div>
```

The Listing 4-22 code is the same as in Listing 4-21, where we create three <div> elements with normal, medium, and large classes assigned to them. Also, we create two <span> elements for creating two tags in each <div> section.

The only difference is in each <div> element, to which we assign the ***tags has-addons*** class to attach the two tags.

The output of the code is shown in Figure 4-22.

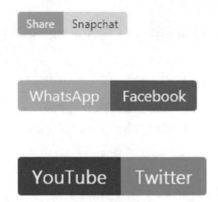

Figure 4-22. *Addons feature attaching two tags*

You can also append the delete button or create a delete tag. Check Listing 4-23.

Listing 4-23. Appending Delete Button and Delete Tag

```
<div class="box">
<div class="tags has-addons are-medium">
<span class="tag is-success">Share</span>
<span class="tag is-warning">Snapchat
<button class="delete"></button>
</span>
</div>
<div class="tags has-addons are-medium">
<span class="tag is-primary">WhatsApp</span>
<span class="tag is-link">Facebook</span>
<a class="tag is-delete"></a>
</div>
```

In Listing 4-23, we create a box container to house two <div> sections where we create medium-sized tags and attach two tags under each <div> element.

To the first <div>, we assign the **tags has-addons** class in conjunction with the **are-medium** class. We create two tags using <span> elements. Then we use a <button> element and assign the **delete** class to it.

For the second <div>, we create two medium-sized attached tags the same way. However, in this <div>, instead of the button element, we use an <a> anchor link tag and assign the **tag is-delete** class to it.

The output of the code is shown in Figure 4-23.

Figure 4-23. *Delete button and delete tag appended, respectively*

You can create a list of tags and group several tags containers together using the **field is-grouped** class for the main <div> container. If the list of tags containers extends more than the 12-column grid, you need to use the **is-grouped-multiline** class as shown in Listing 4-24.

Listing 4-24. Grouped List of Tags with Multiline Output

```
<strong class="box">
<div class="field is-grouped is-grouped-multiline">
  <div class="control">
    <div class="tags has-addons">
      <a class="tag is-success">Data Centers</a>
      <a class="tag is-delete"></a>
    </div>
  </div>
```

```
<div class="control">
  <div class="tags has-addons">
    <a class="tag is-success">Digital transformation</a>
    <a class="tag is-delete"></a>
  </div>
</div>
<div class="control">
  <div class="tags has-addons">
    <a class="tag is-success">Energy-Efficiency</a>
    <a class="tag is-delete"></a>
  </div>
</div>
<div class="control">
  <div class="tags has-addons">
    <a class="tag is-success">Critical Power</a>
    <a class="tag is-delete"></a>
  </div>
</div>
<div class="control">
  <div class="tags has-addons">
    <a class="tag is-success">IT Infrastructure</a>
    <a class="tag is-delete"></a>
  </div>
</div>
<div class="control">
  <div class="tags has-addons">
    <a class="tag is-success">DC Power</a>
    <a class="tag is-delete"></a>
  </div>
</div>
<div class="control">
```

```
    <div class="tags has-addons">
      <a class="tag is-success">Emerson Network Power</a>
      <a class="tag is-delete"></a>
    </div>
  </div>
  <div class="control">
    <div class="tags has-addons">
      <a class="tag is-success">Power Distribution</a>
      <a class="tag is-delete"></a>
    </div>
  </div>
  <div class="control">
    <div class="tags has-addons">
      <a class="tag is-success">Edge Computing</a>
      <a class="tag is-delete"></a>
    </div>
  </div>
  <div class="control">
    <div class="tags has-addons">
      <a class="tag is-success">UPS</a>
      <a class="tag is-delete"></a>
    </div>
  </div>
  <div class="control">
    <div class="tags has-addons">
      <a class="tag is-success">Hyper-Converged Infrastructure</a>
      <a class="tag is-delete"></a>
    </div>
  </div>
 </div>
</strong>
```

In Listing 4-24, we create a box container and create a parent <div> element and assign the *field is-grouped* and the *is-grouped-multiline* classes to it.

Then we create multiple several <div> containers. In each <div> child container, we create subchild <div>s and assign the *control* class to them. Next, we create attached tags using the *tags has-addons class* and create two anchor links, where we create each contextual color tag and append with the delete tag.

We create several <div> elements with the control class, and within them we append two tags using the process mentioned earlier.

The output of the code is shown in Figure 4-24.

Figure 4-24. *Grouped tags container*

The output in Figure 4-24 has a look similar to the tags used in corporate blogs or on the LinkedIn portal among other platforms.

Pagination

Pagination is quite useful in segregation of content in multiple pages and indicates the toggling effect, helping users find the specific content easily. It prevents users from getting overwhelmed with content overload and divides the content into discrete pages, resulting in remarkable readability. Thus, pagination helps reduce complexities and enhances content exploration in a well-organized way.

Bulma has a responsive pagination module, an example of which can be seen in Listing 4-25.

Listing 4-25. Creating a Simple Pagination Module

```
<nav class="pagination" role="navigation">
  <a class="pagination-previous">Previous</a>
  <a class="pagination-next">Next page</a>
  <ul class="pagination-list">
    <li>
      <a class="pagination-link">1</a>
    </li>
    <li>
      <span class="pagination-ellipsis">&hellip;</span>
    </li>
    <li>
      <a class="pagination-link">4</a>
    </li>
    <li>
      <a class="pagination-link is-current">5</a>
    </li>
 </nav>
```

In Listing 4-25, to create the pagination, we initially create a navigation
<nav> element and assign a ***pagination*** class to it. Then we create two
links and assign the ***pagination-previous*** and ***pagination-next*** classes to
it, respectively.

Then we create the pagination buttons by using an unordered list.
The parent <ul> tag is assigned the ***pagination-list*** class. Within the <ul>
element, we create the list items using anchor <a> tags.

First, we create an anchor link <a> and assign the ***pagination-link***
class to it. We also assign the ***is-current*** class to it to make it look like the
current page. We assign 1 as the starting number of the page.

Then we create the second <li> tag and use a <span> element and
assign the ***pagination-ellipsis*** class to it. The ellipsis creates dots, which

is the range separator. Within the <span> tags, we insert the ***…*** to complete the functionality of the ellipsis.

We move on to create the third anchor link tag and assign the ***pagination-link*** class to it and enter the page number as 4. Similarly, we create another pagination list item and name it as 5 for the page number.

The output of the code is shown in Figure 4-25.

Figure 4-25. *Normal pagination*

Bulma has integrated small, medium, and large sizes for the pagination feature shown in Listing 4-26.

Listing 4-26. Creating Different-Sized Pagination Modules

```
<nav class="pagination is-small" role="navigation">
  <a class="pagination-previous">Previous</a>
  <a class="pagination-next">Next page</a>
  <ul class="pagination-list">
    <li>
      <a class="pagination-link">1</a>
    </li>
    <li>
      <span class="pagination-ellipsis">&hellip;</span>
    </li>
    <li>
      <a class="pagination-link">4</a>
    </li>
    <li>
      <a class="pagination-link is-current">5</a>
    </li>
 </nav>
```

```
<br><br>
<nav class="pagination is-medium" role="navigation">
 <a class="pagination-previous">Previous</a>
 <a class="pagination-next">Next page</a>
 <ul class="pagination-list">
   <li>
     <a class="pagination-link">1</a>
   </li>
   <li>
     <span class="pagination-ellipsis">&hellip;</span>
   </li>
   <li>
     <a class="pagination-link">4</a>
   </li>
   <li>
     <a class="pagination-link is-current">5</a>
   </li>
</nav>
<br><br>
<nav class="pagination is-large" role="navigation">
 <a class="pagination-previous">Previous</a>
 <a class="pagination-next">Next page</a>
 <ul class="pagination-list">
   <li>
     <a class="pagination-link">1</a>
   </li>
   <li>
     <span class="pagination-ellipsis">&hellip;</span>
   </li>
   <li>
     <a class="pagination-link">4</a>
```

```
    </li>
    <li>
      <a class="pagination-link is-current">5</a>
    </li>
  </nav>
```

The code example in Listing 4-26 for creating the pagination is the same as in Listing 4-25.

Instead of a single <nav> element, we create three separate <nav> elements. The first <nav> element is assigned the ***pagination is-small*** class (instead of the pagination class in default size) to create a small-sized pagination feature.

For medium-sized and large-sized pagination output, we use the ***pagination is-medium*** and ***pagination is-large*** classes for the second and third <nav> elements, respectively.

The output of the code is shown in Figure 4-26.

Figure 4-26. *Small-, medium-, and large-sized pagination components*

You can change the alignment of the pagination component. You can center it or align it to the right. Apart from that, you can also use the ***disabled*** attribute to disable a link. You can also create rounded pagination components by using the ***is-rounded*** class.

Let's go to Listing 4-27 to understand it better.

Listing 4-27. Pagination Modules with Different Alignment and Rounded Shape

```
<nav class="pagination is-rounded is-right" role="navigation">
  <a class="pagination-previous" disabled>Previous</a>
  <a class="pagination-next">Next page</a>
  <ul class="pagination-list">
    <li>
      <a class="pagination-link is-current">1</a>
    </li>
    <li>
      <span class="pagination-ellipsis">&hellip;</span>
    </li>
    <li>
      <a class="pagination-link">4</a>
    </li>
    <li>
      <a class="pagination-link">5</a>
    </li>
  </ul>
</nav>
<br><hr><br>
<nav class="pagination is-rounded is-centered"
role="navigation">
  <a class="pagination-previous" disabled>Previous</a>
  <a class="pagination-next">Next page</a>
  <ul class="pagination-list">
    <li>
      <a class="pagination-link is-current">1</a>
    </li>
    <li>
      <span class="pagination-ellipsis">&hellip;</span>
    </li>
```

```
  <li>
    <a class="pagination-link">4</a>
  </li>
  <li>
    <a class="pagination-link">5</a>
  </li>
</nav>
```

In Listing 4-27, the process to create the pagination is the same. The specific difference is that for the first <nav> element, we assign the *is-rounded* class in conjunction with the *pagination* class for defining the rounded shape for the pagination component. Thereon, we also assign the *is-right* class, which will align the pagination component to the right of the web page.

Then, in the first <a> element with the *pagination-previous* class, we add the *disabled* attribute to show that the link is disabled. The rest of the code is the same as that for the pagination components in the earlier examples.

Once we are done with the first pagination component, we create the second pagination component using another <nav> element. We assign the pagination *is-rounded* class to this <nav> tag. Here, in conjunction with the *pagination is-rounded* class, we assign an *is-centered* class to align the pagination component to the center. We also use the *disabled* attribute in the first anchor tag akin to the previous navigation element resulting in a grayed-out look for the link.

The rest of the code is the same as that of the first <nav> element or the earlier examples.

The output of the code is shown in Figure 4-27.

Figure 4-27. *Pagination components to the right and center, respectively*

In Figure 4-27, you can see that the first pagination component is aligned to the right. The ***Previous*** & ***Next page*** labels are shifted to the left due to this alignment. In addition, the ***Previous*** label is grayed-out due to the ***disabled*** attribute.

As for the second pagination component, the alignment is to the center. Here, the ***Previous*** & ***Next page*** labels are on opposite ends of the page. Both these screenshots are taken on a tablet-sized screen.

Summary

In this chapter, we looked at navigation elements and media components. In the next chapter, you will learn about buttons, icons, modals, and forms, enabling you to build sophisticated, interactive web pages with ease.

CHAPTER 5

CSS Components and Forms

CSS frameworks have built-in interface elements and components that enable easy and quick development unlike scratch-coding. In this chapter, we will look at useful components like Font Awesome icons, buttons and button-groups, content-wrappers, modals, and forms.

Buttons

Buttons are vital in web design, as they enable the user to interact with your web site, especially in call-to-action scenarios. In modern layouts, you need to follow some basic rules to increase user communication with the buttons. They should prompt the user to click- that's why it should be easy to locate; you should also ensure consistency from an end-user perspective. When it comes to shape, the design should be uniform all throughout the web site (for example, if you are using square buttons, ensure that all the buttons have a square design). However, the size of important buttons can be a bit larger and noticeable. You can use focus and hover functionalities for enhanced usability. An important aspect is that users should get relevant responses once they click the button. For example, you are filling a form, and after entering the required details, you click on Submit. A message stating "Your form has been submitted successfully" or "We have received your application and will get back to you soon" will reassure the user that the required action has been implemented.

Bulma has responsive buttons where you can define different sizes, colors, outlined patterns, display width, shapers, button group, and lists, to mention a few.

Initially, we will look at the different types of buttons in Bulma shown in Listing 5-1.

Listing 5-1. Button Types

```
<a class="button">Link Button</a>
<button class="button">Normal Button</button>
<input class="button" type="submit" value="Submit Input">
<input class="button" type="reset" value="Reset Input">
```

As seen in Listing 5-1, we use an anchor link <a>, <button>, and <input> tags to define buttons. Initially, we use the anchor link <a> tag and use the **button** class to form a button with a link. The <button> tag can be assigned a **button** class to define a button.

In forms, we tend to use the < input> tags. Here, in the first <input> tag, we assign a **button** class in conjunction with the **submit** type attribute. We use the value **Submit Input** as the name of the button.

In the last code line, we use an <input> tag again, to which we also assign the **button** class. We also assign it the **reset** type attribute and set the value as **Reset Input**, which will be the name of the button.

The output of the code is shown in Figure 5-1.

Figure 5-1. *Different button types*

In Figure 5-1, we can see normal buttons as defined in the code.

In Bulma, you can assign a few basic colors as well as the ingrained contextual colors. Listing 5-2 depicts a few of the color buttons in Bulma.

Listing 5-2. Colored Buttons

```
<a class="button is-light">Link Button</a>
<button class="button is-black">Normal Button</button>
<input class="button  is-primary" type="submit" value="Submit
Input">
<input class="button is-warning" type="reset" value="Reset Input">
```

As you can see in Listing 5-2, we have used an anchor link initially and assigned the **button** class in conjunction with the **is-light** color class. For the second button, we use the **button** class in conjunction with the **is-black** color class. The third button using the input tags is assigned the **button** class in conjunction with the **is-primary** class. For the fourth button, we use the **is-warning** class in conjunction with the **button** class.

The output of the code is shown in Figure 5-2.

Figure 5-2. *Few colored buttons*

In Bulma, you can allocate different sizes to the buttons, as shown in Listing 5-3.

Listing 5-3. Different Button Sizes

```
<a class="button is-light is-small">Hyperlink-Button</a>
<button class="button is-black is-normal">Normal Button</button>
<a class="button is-danger">Link</a>
```

```
<input class="button  is-primary is-medium" type="submit"
value="Submit Input">
<input class="button is-warning  is-large" type="reset"
value="Reset Input">
```

Listing 5-3 uses almost the same code as Listing 5-2 except for the size classes. For the first button, we use the **is-small** class, which will result in a small-sized button. For the second button, we use the **is-normal** class, which is the default size. For the third button, we do not use any button size class, as a result of which it will be of normal size just like the second button. In the fourth button code, we use the **is-medium** class, whereas in the fifth button code line, we use the **is-large** class, resulting in medium- and large-sized buttons, respectively.

The output of the code is shown in Figure 5-3.

Figure 5-3. *Different button sizes*

If all the buttons are of the same size, then wrap them in a **buttons** parent using the **buttons are-small**, **buttons are-medium**, and the **buttons are-large** classes depending on the requirement. If you want one button of a different size in a group, you need to assign a different size for only that button in the group as shown in Listing 5-4.

Listing 5-4. Buttons Parent with Buttons, with One Different-Sized Button

```
<div class="buttons are-medium">
  <a class="button is-success">Medium</a>
  <a class="button is-success">Medium</a>
  <a class="button is-success is-normal">Normal</a>
```

```
  <a class="button is-success">Medium</a>
  <a class="button is-success">Medium</a>
  <a class="button is-success">Medium</a>
</div>
```

Listing 5-4 we use a parent <div> element and assign the **buttons are-medium** class to it. This will allocate a medium-size to all the buttons in the group by default. However, in the third line of code, we use the **is-normal** class. As a result, all the buttons will be medium-sized except for the third button, which will end up as a normal sized button owing to the **is-normal** class.

The output of the code is shown in Figure 5-4.

Figure 5-4. *Medium-sized button group with a single, normal-sized button*

Bulma has an outlined feature for its buttons, which will only assign a border for the button, with no color fill-up except for the text. Refer to Listing 5-5 to see an example:

Listing 5-5. Outlined Buttons

```
<a class="button is-outlined is-danger">Link Button</a>
<button class="button is-outlined is-black">Normal Button
</button>
<input class="button is-outlined is-primary" type="submit"
value="Submit Input">
<input class="button is-outlined is-warning" type="reset"
value="Reset Input">
```

In Listing 5-5, we create four buttons. The first button is assigned the **button is-danger** class in conjunction with the **is-outlined** class. The second button is assigned the **button is-black** class in conjunction with the **is-outlined** class. The third button is assigned the **button is-primary** class in tandem with the **is-outlined** class. The fourth button is assigned the button **is-warning** class alongside the **is-outlined** class.

The output of the code is shown in Figure 5-5.

Figure 5-5. *Outlined buttons*

Bulma offers a full-width class, using which the button can stretch to the full-width screen as shown in Listing 5-6.

Listing 5-6. Full-Width Buttons

```
<a class="button is-primary is-small is-fullwidth">SMALL</a>
   <br><br>
   <a class="button is-info is-normal is-fullwidth">Default</a>
   <br><br>
   <a class="button is-danger is-medium is-fullwidth">Medium</a>
   <br><br>
   <a class="button is-warning is-large is-fullwidth">Large</a>
```

In Listing 5-6, we create four buttons. For the first button, we use the **button is-primary** class in conjunction with the **is-small** and **is-fullwidth** classes. The second button has been assigned the **button is-info** contextual color class in conjunction with the **is-normal** and **is-fullwidth** classes. The third button is created using the **button is-danger** class in conjunction with the **is-medium** and **is-fullwidth** classes. The last button is assigned the **button is-warning** class in conjunction with the **is-large** and **is-fullwidth** classes.

The output of the code is shown in Figure 5-6.

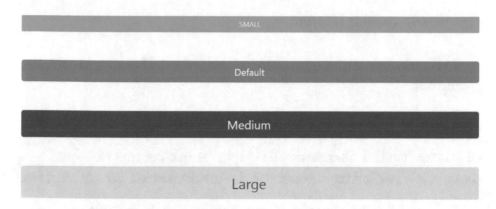

Figure 5-6. *Full-width different size buttons*

In Figure 5-6, we see that the buttons have the size and contextual colors assigned in the code. All four buttons stretch to the full-width of the screen, as defined in the code.

Bulma also has an ingrained inverted class. The inverted feature takes the color defined for the button and applies it to the text without any fill-up for that button color, as shown in Listing 5-7.

Listing 5-7. Inverted Feature

```
<button class="button is-black is-inverted">Submit</button>
<button class="button is-info is-inverted">Sign-Up</button>
<button class="button is-danger is-inverted">Cancel</button>
<button class="button is-primary is-inverted">Login</button>
```

Listing 5-7 assigns the black, info, danger, and primary colors to the buttons in conjunction with the **is-inverted** class. As a result, we get buttons where the text color for that button is same as that of the color classes, except that the buttons are not colored as defined in the code.

Submit   Sign-Up   Cancel   Login

Figure 5-7. *Inverted feature*

In Bulma, you can assign a rounded shape for the buttons, as shown in Listing 5-8.

Listing 5-8. Rounded Buttons

```
<a class="button is-rounded is-light">Link Button</a>
<button class="button is-rounded is-black">Normal Button</button>
```

In Listing 5-8, we create two buttons and assign the **is-light** and **is-black** classes in conjunction with the **is-rounded** class respectively. This will result in a rounded border to the buttons as shown in Figure 5-8.

Link Button   Normal Button

Figure 5-8. *Rounded buttons*

You can also assign the hover functionality, which will highlight the button, when you hover over it. In addition, you can also use the focus functionality, which will highlight that button in the code output. Bulma has an active feature, which will display the button as the selected one.

You can also create a static button, which can be used in conjunction with a form label—commonly used in form design in modern layouts. In Bulma, you can also assign an intermediate loading display style to the buttons.

Listing 5-9 shows an example of all these functionalities.

Listing 5-9. Focus, Hover, Static, and Buffering (Loading) Status

```
<a class="button is-focused">Button</a>
<br><br>
<a class="button is-hovered">Button</a>
<br> <br>
<a class="button is-active">Button</a>
<br> <br>
<a class="button is-static">Button</a>
<br> <br>
<a class="button is-primary is-loading">Button</a>
```

In Listing 5-9, we create five buttons. We use the **is-focused**, **is-hovered**, **is-active**, **is-static**, and **is-loading** classes to show the five functionalities. The output of the code is shown in Figure 5-9.

Figure 5-9. *Focus, hover, active, static, and buffering buttons*

Bulma helps you group buttons on a single line using the field container and the is-grouped modifier, as shown in Listing 5-10.

Listing 5-10. Grouping Buttons on a Single Line

```
<div class="field is-grouped">
  <p class="control">
    <a class="button is-link">
      Login
    </a>
  </p>
  <p class="control">
    <a class="button is-warning">
      Sign-Up
    </a>
  </p>
  <p class="control">
    <a class="button is-danger">
      GitHub
    </a>
  </p>
</div>
```

In Listing 5-10, we create a parent <div> element and assign it the **field** and **is-grouped** classes. Next, we create three <p> paragraph tags. Inside each <p> element, we create three buttons and assign the link, warning, and danger contextual colors to each of them, respectively.

The output of the code is seen in Figure 5-10.

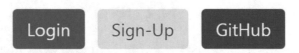

Figure 5-10. *Grouping buttons in a single line*

You can also connect two buttons with each other as addons. We use the same code as in Listing 5-10, except that we add a **has-addons** modifier to the parent field container as shown in Listing 5-11.

Listing 5-11. Addons Combining Three Buttons

```
<div class="field has-addons">
  <p class="control">
    <a class="button is-link">
      Login
    </a>
  </p>
  <p class="control">
    <a class="button is-warning">
      Sign-Up
    </a>
  </p>
  <p class="control">
    <a class="button is-danger">
      GitHub
    </a>
  </p>
</div>
```

From the preceding listing, all we have done is add the **has-addons** class to the **field** class.

The output of the code is shown in Figure 5-11.

Figure 5-11. *Addons button implementation*

In Bulma, you can also create button lists. If the button list contains a lot of buttons exceeding the default 12-column grid space, then it will wrap on multiple lines with equal spacing between all buttons.

In Listing 5-12, we use the **buttons** class with the <div> element and then define a list of buttons of different colors using the <span> tags. Therefore, the buttons will be displayed in a line.

Listing 5-12. Buttons List

```
<div class="buttons">
  <span class="button is-success">Login</span>
  <span class="button is-info">Sign-up</span>
  <span class="button is-danger">Send</span>
  <span class="button is-success">Login</span>
  <span class="button is-info">Sign-up</span>
  <span class="button is-danger">Send</span>
  <span class="button is-success">Login</span>
  <span class="button is-info">Sign-up</span>
  <span class="button is-danger">Send</span>
  <span class="button is-success">Login</span>
  <span class="button is-info">Sign-up</span>
  <span class="button is-danger">Send</span>
  <span class="button is-success">Login</span>
  <span class="button is-info">Sign-up</span>
  <span class="button is-danger">Send</span>
```

The output of the code is shown in Figure 5-12.

Figure 5-12. *Button list wrapping on multiple lines (Tablet Screen)*

In Figure 5-12, we can see that the buttons are in a single line; on exceeding the space of one row, they continue in the next line.

Note: This screenshot was taken using a tablet screen.

So far, we have seen the different button-based aspects; in the next section, we take a look at Bulma's compatible icons.

Icons

Icons are important in web design from a readability point of view. You can draw the user's attention using icons due to their aesthetical attribute. For example, a danger sign icon will alert the user about some untoward action; for instance, an antivirus blocks access to some malicious web site or virus-laden portal, and shows a danger sign alerting you to refrain from surfing that web site. It also helps if the danger icon is accompanied with relevant text.

Bulma displays excellent compatibility with Font Awesome icons, Material Design icons, and Open Iconic icons. The latest Bulma release is compatible with the Font Awesome 5.x version and we will learn it in detail.

In Bulma, you can add contextual and built-in color modifiers for icons, as the icon fonts are always fonts. Let's understand it better using a code sample in Listing 5-13.

Listing 5-13. Icons with Different Contextual Colors

```
<span class="icon has-text-info">
  <i class="fas fa-share-alt-square"></i>
</span>
<span class="icon">
  <i class="fas fa-share-alt-square"></i>
</span>
```

```
<span class="icon has-text-success">
  <i class="fas fa-share-alt-square"></i>
</span>
<span class="icon has-text-warning">
  <i class="fas fa-share-alt-square"></i>
</span>
```

In Listing 5-13, we use four <span> elements. For each <span> tag, we use the **icon** class to define the icon container. We use **has-text-info**, **has-text-square**, and **has-text-warning** classes for the first, third, and fourth <span> tags, whereas no text color modifier is added for the second icon. To create an icon, we use Font Awesome and include the **fas fa-share-alt-square** class, which is an icon for Share, like you usually see in social media sites nowadays (fas is the common syntax for all Font Awesome icons, whereas the type of icon is defined by the latter icon type).

The output of the code is shown in Figure 5-13.

Figure 5-13. *Same icon—different colors*

Bulma allows you to have icons of different sizes, with an additional capability to magnify the size using multipliers as shown in Listing 5-14.

Listing 5-14. Icons with Different Sizes and Magnifiers

```
<span class="icon is-medium has-text-danger">
  <i class="fas fa-share-alt-square"></i>
</span>
<span class="icon is-medium has-text-danger">
  <i class="fas fa-2x fa-share-alt-square"></i>
</span>
```

```
<br><br>
<span class="icon is-large has-text-success">
  <i class="fas fa-share-alt-square"></i>
</span>
<span class="icon is-large has-text-success">
  <i class="fas fa-2x fa-share-alt-square"></i>
</span>
<span class="icon is-large has-text-success">
  <i class="fas fa-3x fa-share-alt-square"></i>
</span>
```

In Listing 5-14, we club the **icon is-medium** and **has-text-danger** classes together. We use the Font Awesome Share icon. In the next <span> tag, we use the same code but we also add a magnifier **fa-2x** to magnify that icons size.

Similarly, we create three more <span> tags in the next line where we use the **icon is-large** class and **has-text-success** classes together. We define a Font Awesome Share icon using the **fa-share-alt-square** class. Then we keep the first icon as the default large size but add **fa-2x** and **fa-3x** classes to magnify the large icon size

The output of the code is shown in Figure 5-14, where you can see the desired magnifying effect. Below the code output is the table of Bulma's Font Awesome icon-based different sizes and magnifiers.

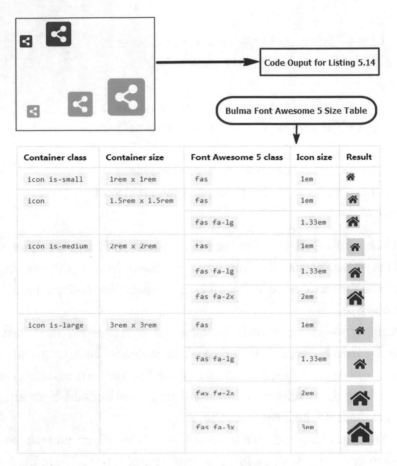

Container class	Container size	Font Awesome 5 class	Icon size	Result
icon is-small	1rem x 1rem	fas	1em	
icon	1.5rem x 1.5rem	fas	1em	
		fas fa-lg	1.33em	
icon is-medium	2rem x 2rem	fas	1em	
		fas fa-lg	1.33em	
		fas fa-2x	2em	
icon is-large	3rem x 3rem	fas	1em	
		fas fa-lg	1.33em	
		fas fa-2x	2em	
		fas fa-3x	3em	

Figure 5-14. *Code output of different icon sizes and magnifiers, along with Font Awesome 5 size table*

In Bulma, if you define a button that contains only an icon, the button will be square regardless of the size of the button or icon. Refer to Listing 5-15.

Listing 5-15. Button with Only an Icon

```
<a class="button is-large">
  <div class="icon is-large">
    <i class="fas fa-share-alt-square"></i>
  </div>
  </a>
  <br><br>
  <a class="button is-large">
    <div class="icon is-large">
      <i class="fas fa-share-alt-square fa-2x"></i>
    </div>
  </a>
  <br><br>
  <a class="button is-large">
    <div class="icon is-large">
      <i class="fas fa-share-alt-square fa-3x"></i>
    </div>
  </a>
```

In Listing 5-15, we create three buttons using the <a> anchor link tags and assign the button **is-large** class for all of them. We then create a Font Awesome Share icon. For the first button, we keep it as it is by default. The second button and third button are assigned the **fa-2x** and **fa-3x** magnifier classes respectively.

The output of the code is shown in Figure 5-15.

Figure 5-15. *Button with only an icon*

In Figure 5-15, we can see that the three buttons are square, irrespective of the size of the button or icons.

Bulma also allows you to use buttons with icons appended with the button text, as shown in Listing 5-16.

Listing 5-16. Buttons with Incorporated Icons

```
<p class="buttons">
  <a class="button is-info">
    <span class="icon">
    <i class="fab fa-facebook-messenger"></i>
    </span>
    <span>Messenger</span>
  </a>
  <a class="button is-primary">
    <span class="icon">
    <i class="fab fa-twitter-square"></i>
    </span>
    <span>Twitter</span>
  </a>
```

```
<a class="button is-danger">
  <span class="icon is-small">
   <i class="fab fa-pinterest"></i>
  </span>
  <span>Pinterest</span>
</a>
<a class="button is-link is-outlined">
  <span>Reddit</span>
  <span class="icon is-small">
   <i class="fab fa-reddit-alien"></i>
  </span>
</a>
<a class="button is-warning">
  <span>SnapChat</span>
  <span class="icon is-small">
   <i class="fab fa-snapchat-ghost"></i>
  </span>
</a>
</p>
```

In Listing 5-16, we create a group of buttons. We do that using a **buttons** group class container with the <p> element. We create five buttons. For the first button, we define an anchor tag <a> and assign it the **button is-info** class. Within the <a> tag, we use a <span> tag and assign the **icon** class to it. Then we create an <i> tag where we define the Facebook messenger icon. Moving forward, we create another <span> tag and define the name of the button as Messenger.

Similarly, we use four more buttons using similar code, except that the icons are different and assigned a name as per the social media context—namely, Twitter, Pinterest, Reddit, and Snapchat.

The output of the code is shown in Figure 5-16.

Figure 5-16. *Buttons with Icons*

In Figure 5-16, we can see that the icons are depicted with the button text as defined in the code.

Now that you are acquainted with icons, we will look at the content class feature in the next section.

Content Wrapper

There are instances when you cannot use CSS classes. In those scenarios, you stick to HTML markup; also, at times you need to use HTML tags only for some text. Bulma's content element is just what's needed in such situations as it is a container for any type of content. For example, if you use HTML tags for unordered lists, you can enclose the code inside an element with the content class.

For ordered lists, you can either use the respective HTML attribute value or CSS modifier class.

For example, if we use the **type** attribute and specify the attribute value as 1, then it will show an ordered list with the numbers 1, 2, 3…and so on. For type value as A, it will show the ordered list as A, B, C… and so on. Similarly, you can define lower character roman letters (i, ii, iii, etc.), uppercase Roman letters (I, II, III, etc.), and lower case alphabets (a, b, c, etc.), using **i**, **I**, and **a** as the type attribute values, respectively.

The other method is to use CSS modifiers like is-lower-alpha, and so on.

Let's understand the HTML type attribute better from a code example in Listing 5-17.

Listing 5-17. Ordered Lists Within the Content Container

```
<ol type="1">
    <li>Yes</li>
    <li>No</li>
    <li>Maybe</li>
</ol>
<ol type="A">
    <li>Yes</li>
    <li>No</li>
    <li>Maybe</li>
</ol>
<ol type="a">
    <li>Yes</li>
    <li>No</li>
    <li>Maybe</li>
</ol>
<ol type="I">
    <li>Yes</li>
    <li>No</li>
    <li>Maybe</li>
</ol>
<ol type="i">
    <li>Yes</li>
    <li>No</li>
    <li>Maybe<//
</ol>
```

In Listing 5-17, we use a parent <div> element and assign the **content** class to it (making it a content wrapper). For the first ordered list defined within the <ol> tags, we assign **1** as the value of the **type** attribute. Next, we define the list items using the <li> tags. For the first ordered lists defined within the <ol> tags, we assign **1** as the value of the **type** attribute. Next, we define the list items using the <li> tags.

For the second ordered list defined within the <ol> tags, we assign **A** as the value of the **type** attribute. Next, we define the list items using the <li> tags. For the third ordered list defined within the <ol> tags, we assign **a** as the value of the **type** attribute. Next, we define the list items using the <li> tags. Similarly, for the fourth and fifth ordered list, we use **I** and **I** as the **type** attribute values respectively.

The output of the code is shown in Figure 5-17.

1. Yes

2. No

3. Maybe

A. Yes

B. No

C. Maybe

a. Yes

b. No

c. Maybe

I. Yes

II. No

III. Maybe

i. Yes

ii. No

iii. Maybe

Figure 5-17. *Ordered lists within the content wrapper*

Therefore, the content wrapper is used to handle *WYSIWYG*-generated content, specifically where HTML tags are used.

In the next section, we will touch base with modals, which are quite handy at times in modern layouts.

Modals

Modals are basically overlays, essential a float on the web page. Modals are used in the following situations: to collect data, prompt users (alerts & warnings), get user input, or as an intermediary before displaying important content, features, or update announcements.

Though modals are quite useful in grabbing the user's attention, they should be used sparingly because they distract the user's focus from the main content. Therefore, it is better to restrict their use to mission-critical data/information or step-by-step wizards. Nevertheless, they save significant UI screen estate, while also being decisive. You should not cram too much content in the modal body, meaning it should be precise and entice the user toward a specific call-to-action. Keep them minimalistic.

Bulma has an intuitive modal component that can be used for diverse use cases; it helps retain user-focus on the context of the current screen without interrupting the workflow. We will see two code examples, one of which is a content modal and the other an image modal.

Listing 5-18 is an example of a content modal. One important thing to note is that Bulma is purely CSS and to trigger a modal action, we have to use a bit of JavaScript.

Listing 5-18. Content Modal

```
<button class="button is-success modal-button" data-
target="#myModal" aria-haspopup="true"> <b>Content Modal Click
</b></button>

<div class="modal" id="myModal">
  <div class="modal-background"></div>
```

```
  <div class="modal-content">

   <p class="box">
   Havana brown. Malkin......
   </p>

  </div>
  <button class="modal-close is-large" aria-label="close"></button>
</div>
 <script>
          document.querySelectorAll('.modal-button').
          forEach(function(el) {
  el.addEventListener('click', function() {
    var target = document.querySelector(el.getAttribute('data-
    target'));

    target.classList.add('is-active');

    target.querySelector('.modal-close').
    addEventListener('click',   function() {
        target.classList.remove('is-active');
      });
   });
 });
});
</script>
```

In Listing 5-18, we first create a modal trigger button, which on being clicked, will display the modal. We assign a **modal** class to the <button> tag and assign the **is-success** contextual color to it; we define a **modal-button** class for it too. Then we use a **data-target** value as **#myModal**, which will be used for the JavaScript purposes. We name the modal button **Content Modal Click**.

Next, we create a <div> class, assign the **modal** class to it, and assign the **id** as **myModal**, which in turn was the value of the **data-target** value mentioned earlier.

Within the parent <div>, we create a child <div> and assign the **modal-background** class to it and then use a closing <div> tag. Then we create the second <div> child under the parent <div> and assign the **modal-content** class to it.

Then we create a paragraph tag and assign the **box** class to it. Post closure of the parent <div> element, we move on to create a large button and assign the **modal-close** class to it. Now we write the JavaScript code.

Here, the document.querySelectorAll('.modal-button') method matches all the elements in the DOM (Document Object Model) that has the 'modal-button' class. Next, we loop through these list of elements with a forEach method and apply a callback function to each of the element that matches that class. When the callback function is applied on each of the DOM elements, it adds an event listener with another callback that would run when that event is triggered.

To explain it further, when there is a click event on any DOM element with the class, 'modal-button', a callback is triggered that gets all the element with the 'data-target' attribute. When this happens, we add an 'is-active' class to that element to signify that we want it to become active.

On the other hand, we then target the DOM element with the 'modal-close' class and add an event listener to handle when a user clicks on it. When this happens, we trigger a callback, which helps us to remove/reset the 'is-active' class from the modal.

Remember that the entire JavaScript code must come within the <script> before the closing <body> tag. When we execute the code, we can see a **Content Modal Click** button. On clicking the button, the modal is displayed over the screen.

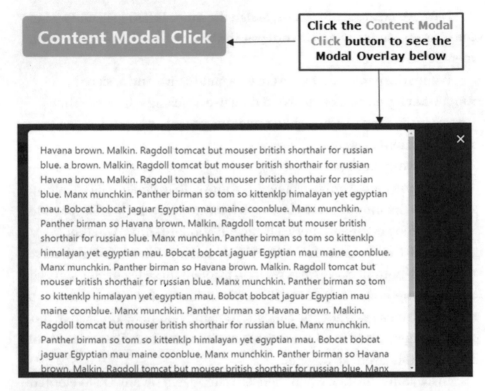

Figure 5-18. *Content modal*

For an image modal, the entire code style is similar, including the JavaScript code. All we do is replace the content within the <div>, to which we have assigned the **modal-content** class. We use the **image** container and **is-4by3** as the ratio modifier. The rest of the code is the same as that of the content modal. Refer to Listing 5-19, which highlights the code that is different. Also, the name of the trigger modal button is changed to **Café Modal**.

Listing 5-19. Image Modal

```
<button class="button is-link modal-button" data-
target="#myModal" aria-haspopup="true"><strong> Cafe Modal
</strong></button>
```

```html
<div class="modal" id="myModal">
  <div class="modal-background"></div>
  <div class="modal-content">
  <p class="image is-4by3">
  <img src="Images/Coffee-Shop-PixaBay.png" alt="Coffee-Shop-
  PixaBay">
  </p>
  </div>
  <button class="modal-close is-large" aria-label="close">
  </button>
</div>
 <script>
    document.querySelectorAll('.modal-button').
    forEach(function(el) {
  el.addEventListener('click', function() {
    var target = document.querySelector(el.getAttribute
    ('data-target'));

    target.classList.add('is-active');

    target.querySelector('.modal-close').addEventListener
    ('click',   function() {
       target.classList.remove('is-active');
     });
  });
});
});
</script>
```

The output of the code will show a **Café Modal** button; clicking it will display an image modal on top of the web page (Figure 5-19).

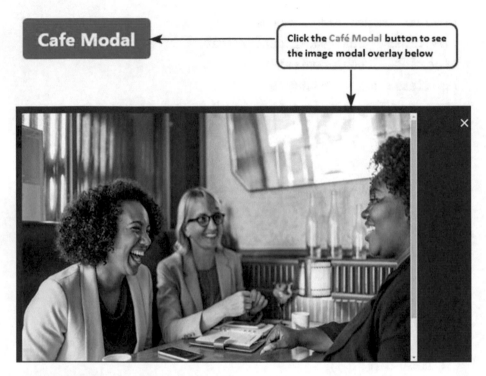

Figure 5-19. *Image modal*

After getting to grips with the modal design, we will now move to forms—a common feature in web designing projects.

Forms

Forms are a useful utility that allows users to enter data; the collected data is then sent to the servers for processing purposes. The concept of displaying e-mail addresses on the web site is quite redundant due to phishing or spam bulk mail among other concerns. Thus, web site owners prefer a contact form. Bulma's forms components are flexible and easy-to-use. In this section, we will look at the procedure of building form fields in an easy-to-follow way.

Initially, we will look at how to create a form field with a label, as shown in Listing 5-20. We will also see different sizes of form fields.

Listing 5-20. Form Fields with Different Sizes

```
<div class="field">
<label class="label is-small">Label</label>
 <div class="control">
<input class="input is-small" type="text" placeholder="Small-
sized Label & Input">
  </div>
            <br>
 <div class="field">
<label class="label">Label</label>
   <div class="control">
<input class="input" type="text" placeholder="Normal-sized
Label & Input">
   </div>
</div>
            <br>
 <div class="field">
<label class="label is-medium">Label</label>
 <div class="control">
<input class="input is-medium" type="text" placeholder="Medium-
sized Label & Input">
   </div>
</div>
            <br>
<div class="field">
<label class="label is-large">Label</label>
<div class="control">
```

```
<input class="input is-large" type="text" placeholder="Large-
sized Label & Input">
 </div>
</div>
```

> *Before explaining the code, remember that all the form control classes should be wrapped in a .control container. While combining many form controls, the .field class should be used as a container to maintain equal spacing.*

Since we are writing the code for four different form fields in Listing 5-20, we will start with a <div> element and assign the **field** class to it. For the first form field, we create a <label> tag and assign the **label is-small** class to it. We then define the input characteristics. For the <input> tag, we assign the **input is-small** class and **type** as **text**. We assign a placeholder for the form field using the **placeholder** attribute.

For the second form field, we use similar code, but we just enter **label** as the class for the <label> tag and **input** as the class for the <input> tag.

For the third, medium-sized form field, we again use similar code but we assign the **label is-medium** class for the <label> tag and **input is-medium** class for the <input> tag.

For the large-sized form field, we use similar code but we assign the **label is-large** class for the <label> tag and **input is-large** for the <input> tag.

For all the tags, as mentioned in the first form field, we use a placeholder.

The output of the code is shown in Figure 5-20.

Label

Small-sized Label & Input

Label

Normal-sized Label & Input

Label

Medium-sized Label & Input

Label

Large-sized Label & Input

Figure 5-20. *Different sizes of form fields*

Bulma enables you to use addons to attach controls together. In the next example in Listing 5-21, we use addons where we combine buttons with form fields. We can also align the controls to the right, center, and even extend to full width.

Listing 5-21. Control Attached with Addons and Diverse Alignment

```
<div class="field has-addons">
<div class="control">
<input class="input" type="text" placeholder="Enter Search Query">
</div>
<div class="control">
<a class="button is-static"> Search </a>
</div>
</div>
          <br><br>
<div class="field has-addons has-addons-right">
```

```
<div class="control">
<input class="input" type="text" placeholder="Enter Search
Query">
</div>
<div class="control">
<a class="button is-static">Search </a>
</div>
</div>
        <br><br>
<div class="field has-addons has-addons-centered">
<div class="control">
<input class="input" type="text" placeholder="Enter Search
Query">
</div>
<div class="control">
<a class="button is-static"> Search </a>
</div>
</div>
              <br><br>
<div class="field has-addons">
<div class="control is-expanded">
<input class="input" type="text" placeholder="Enter Search
Query">
</div>
<div class="control">
<a class="button is-static"> Search </a>
</p>
</div>
</div>
```

In Listing 5-21, we create four addons form control fields.

For the first form field, we create a parent <div> and assign the **field has-addons** class to it. Then we create a child <div> and assign the **control** class to it. Within an <input> tag, we assign the **input** class, **type** as **text**, and a placeholder. Then we create the second child <div> and assign the **control** class to it. We then define a static button using the **button is-static** class and assign the **Search** name to it. This will combine the form field with the static button.

For the second form field, we use the same code; but in this case, the only difference is that we assign the **has-addons-right** class in conjunction with the **field has-addons** class. This will result in alignment of the form field to the right-side.

Similarly, we create the third form field; we use the same code but here we use the **has-addons-centered** class in conjunction with the **field has-addons** class.

As for the fourth form field, we create a full-width form field by using the **is-expanded** class in conjunction with the **control** class for the first child <div> in that section. The rest of the code is same as that of the first form field.

The output of the code is shown in Figure 5-21.

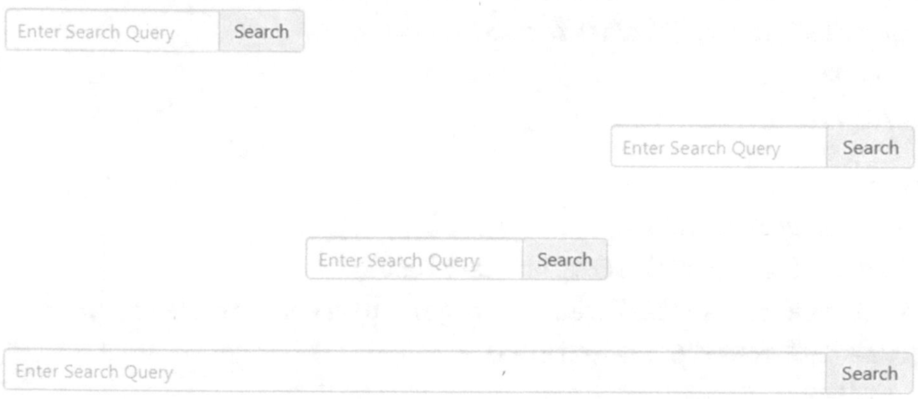

Figure 5-21. *Form fields with addons with diverse alignment*

In the preceding screen-shot, the first form field with the static Search button is aligned to the left by default, the second aligned to the right, the third aligned to the center, and the fourth a full-width form field—each with a static **Search** button.

We can also create a text area in Bulma, which will be able to encompass quite a lot of content as shown in Listing 5-22. We can also assign a buffering or loading feature in the form fields, which is also shown in this listing.

Listing 5-22. Creating a Text Area Box and Rounded Form Field

```
<div class="field">
<label class="label">Name</label>
<div class="control is-loading">
<input class="input is-rounded" type="text">
  </div>
  </div>
                <br>
 <div class="field">
<label class="label">Remarks</label>
<textarea class="textarea is-success" placeholder="Enter your
comments" rows="3"></textarea>
  </div>
  </div>

<br>
<div class="field">
<label class="label">Complaints</label>
<textarea class="textarea is-danger" placeholder="Enter your
comments" rows="6"></textarea>
   </div>
   </div>
```

In Listing 5-22, we create a Name form field the usual way. But after defining the label, we assign the **is-loading** class to the **control** class for the <div> element. Then, we use an <input> tag, and assign the **input is-rounded** class and **type** as **text**.

Now that we have created the first rounded form field, we move on to the next part where we create two text area boxes. For the first text area box, we use a parent <div> with the **field** class and create a label for the text area box. Next, we use the <textarea> tag and assign the **textarea** class to it. We move on to add the **is-success** color modifier to this box and define the placeholder. Next, we define the number of rows as **3** using the rows attribute.

For the second textarea box, we use the same code, but here we give it a danger contextual color modifier instead of the success color modifier in the first. We also define the number of rows as **6**.

The output of the code on a tablet is shown in Figure 5-22.

Figure 5-22. *Rounded form field and different sized and colored text area boxes*

In Figure 5-22, we can see that the first form field has a rounded border. At the right of the form field, you can see the loading status state.

The text-area boxes with a 3-row size and 6-row size with their respective colors are also displayed below the form field.

Moving forward, we will learn about the drop-down menu functionality in forms, as shown in Listing 5-23.

Listing 5-23. Creating a Drop-Down Select Field

```
<div class="field has-addons">
  <div class="control">
    <div class="select is-fullwidth">
      <select name="Engineering courses">
      <option value="Electrical Engineering">Electrical
      Engineering</option>
      <option value="Architectural Engineering">Architectural
      Engineering</option>
      <option value="Automotive Engineering">Automotive
      Engineering</option>
      <option value="Aerospace Engineering">Aerospace
      Engineering</option>
      <option value="Mechanical Engineering">Mechanical
      Engineering</option>
      <option value="Computer Engineering">Computer Engineering
      </option>
      <option value="Robotics Engineering">Robotics Engineering
      </option>
      <option value="Chemical Engineering">Chemical Engineering
      </option>
      <option value="Engineering Management">Engineering
      Management</option>
```

```
        <option value="Industrial Engineering">Industrial
        Engineering</option>
          </select>
        </div>
      </div>
      <div class="control">
        <button type="submit" class="button is-static">Select your
        Course</button>
      </div>
    </div>
```

In Listing 5-23, we create a parent <div> and assign the **field** class to it. Then we create a control by assigning the **control** class to the child <div>. Within this child <div> we create another child <div> and assign the **select** class to it in conjunction with the **is-fullwidth** class. Then we create a <select> tag and assign a name to it.

Then, we create drop-down menu items using the <option> tags. For each <option> tag, we assign a value that is the name of the menu item. Once we are done, after the closing <div> element, we create a <div> element, which is the second child of the main <div> element at the start, and create a button and assign the **is-static** class to it.

The output of the code is a form field with a static button and drop-down. On clicking the drop-down icon, you can see the different fields in the drop-down menu, as shown in Figure 5-23.

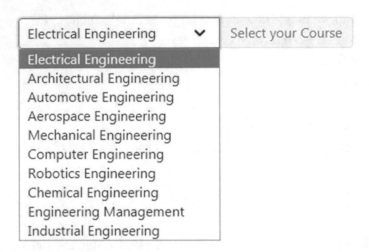

Figure 5-23. *Dropdown menu items shown after clicking the drop-down icon*

Now, if you want the drop-down to be shown directly without clicking the drop-down icon, you need to make a minor modification in the code as shown in Listing 5-24.

Listing 5-24. Direct Dropdown Menu Displayed upon Code Execution

```
<div class="field has-addons">
  <div class="control">
    <div class="select is-fullwidth">
      <select multiple size="10" name="Engineering courses">
      <option value="Electrical Engineering">Electrical
      Engineering</option>
      <option value="Architectural Engineering">Architectural
      Engineering</option>
      <option value="Automotive Engineering">Automotive
      Engineering</option>
      <option value="Aerospace Engineering">Aerospace
      Engineering</option>
```

```
<option value="Mechanical Engineering">Mechanical
Engineering</option>
<option value="Computer Engineering">Computer Engineering
</option>
<option value="Robotics Engineering">Robotics Engineering
</option>
<option value="Chemical Engineering">Chemical Engineering
</option>
<option value="Engineering Management">Engineering
Management</option>
<option value="Industrial Engineering">Industrial
Engineering</option>
  </select>
 </div>
</div>
<div class="control">
 <button type="submit" class="button is-static">Select your
 Course</button>
</div>
</div>
```

In Listing 5-24, the code is almost the same, but we use an attribute, **multiple size**, and assign the value **10** to it, meaning it will display ten items in the drop-down without the need to click the drop-down icon.

In Figure 5-24, the menu items in the drop-down are shown by default without the need to click the drop-down icon.

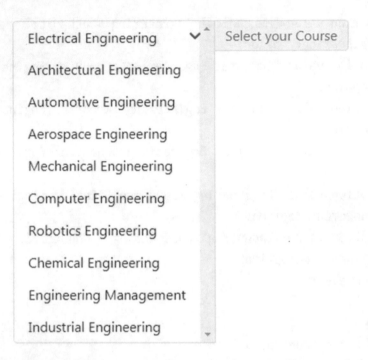

Figure 5-24. *Dropdown menu shown automatically on code output*

Now that we have seen several form components, let's build a Sign-Up form, which you come across in real-time scenarios.

Listing 5-25 shows the initial code of a sign up form, using which you can design the Name and Email fields.

Listing 5-25. Creating the Name and Email Fields

```
<h3 class="title"> <b>Sign Up </b></h3>
 <div class="field">
  <label class="label">Name</label>
  <div class="control">
    <input class="input" type="text" placeholder="Joe Black">
  </div>
  <br>
```

```
<div class="field">
 <label class="label">Email</label>
 <div class="control has-icons-left has-icons-right">
   <input class="input is-danger" type="email"
   placeholder="jone.black@potterlogic.com">
   <span class="icon is-small is-left">
     <i class="fas fa-envelope"></i>
   </span>
   <span class="icon is-small is-right">
     <i class="fas fa-exclamation-triangle"></i>
   </span>
 </div>
 <p class="help is-danger">Do you mean joe.black@potterlogic.com</p>
</div>

<div class="field">
  <label class="label"></label>
  <div class="control has-icons-left has-icons-right">
    <input class="input" type="email" placeholder="Re-enter
    your Email" >
    <span class="icon is-small is-left">
      <i class="fas fa-envelope"></i>
    </span>
    <span class="icon is-small is-right">
      <i class="fas fa-exclamation-triangle"></i>
    </span>
  </div>
  <p class="help is-danger"></p>
</div>
</div>
```

In Listing 5-25, we create the heading for the form using the <h3> tag and name it **Sign Up**.

Then, we create the Name form field the usual way: we create a <div> element and assign the **field** class to it. Then, we create a label by using the **label** class with the <label> tag. Next we create a child <div> and assign the **control** class to it. Then we define the <input> tag and assign the **input** class and **type** value as **text** along with a placeholder.

Next, we create the Email form field. Just like the Name form field, we create a <div> element and assign the **field** class to it. Then we create a label called Email. But here, once we define the Email label, we create a child <div> and assign the **control** class in conjunction with the **has-icons-left** and **has-icons-right** classes. This feature will place icons to the left and right as defined later in the code.

Then we create an <input> tag and assign the **input** class in conjunction with the **is-danger** contextual color; we define the **type** value as email here. Then we define two icons. We create the mail icon using the **fas fa-envelope** class within the first <span> tag. We also assign the **is-small** and **is-left** class to it; this will result in a smaller size icon and pull the icon to the left of the form field. Next, we define another icon using a different <span> tag and assign the **is-small** and **is-right** classes to it. The icon here would be an exclamation triangle. As defined, the icon will be of smaller size and pushed to the right of the form field. Then we create a paragraph <p> element and assign the **help is-danger** class to it along with the message "**Do you mean joe.black@potterlogic.com**."

Similarly, we create another Email field but we do not define a label for it. The placeholder here will be **Re-enter your Email**. The rest of the code is the same as that of the Email field.

The output of the code is shown in Figure 5-25.

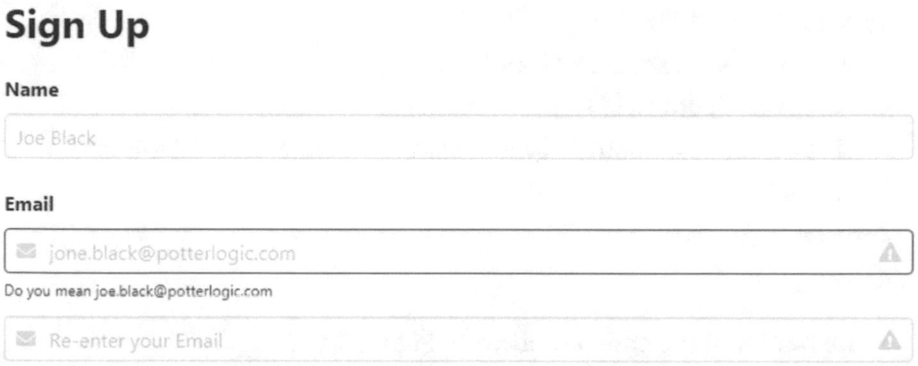

Sign Up

Name

Joe Black

Email

✉ jone.black@potterlogic.com   ⚠

Do you mean joe.black@potterlogic.com

✉ Re-enter your Email   ⚠

Figure 5-25. *Name, email, and reenter email fields*

Then we define the Password section. Here we use similar code as that of the Name form field. We create a **field** container and define the label as **Password**. Then we create a <div> element and assign the **control** class to it. We create an <input> tag and assign the **input** class to it. The **type** here would be text, and thereon we define the placeholder text.

Similarly, we create another Password just like the preceding password form field for the purpose of re-entering the password.

The code snippet for this is shown in Listing 5-26.

Listing 5-26. Creating the Password Form Fields

```
<div class="field">
  <label class="label">Password</label>
  <div class="control">
    <input class="input" type="text" placeholder="Enter
    Password">
  </div>
</div>
```

```
<div class="field">
  <label class="label"></label>
  <div class="control">
    <input class="input" type="text" placeholder="Re-Enter
    Password">
  </div>
</div>
```

The output of the code is shown in Figure 5-26.

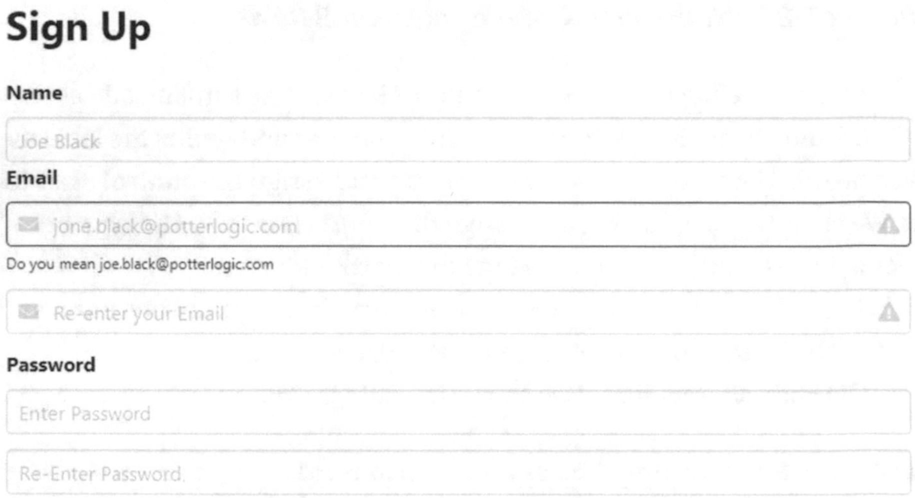

Sign Up

Name

Joe Black

Email

jone.black@potterlogic.com

Do you mean joe.black@potterlogic.com

Re-enter your Email

Password

Enter Password

Re-Enter Password

Figure 5-26. *Password fields added in the sign up form*

Next, we create an **Upload** button for uploading files, as shown in Listing 5-27.

Listing 5-27. Upload Button

```
<div class="field">
  <div class="file is-primary">
    <label class="file-label">
      <input class="file-input" type="file" name="resume">
```

```
    <span class="file-cta">
      <span class="file-icon">
        <i class="fas fa-upload"></i>
      </span>
      <span class="file-label">
        Click-to-Upload
      </span>
    </span>
  </label>
 </div>
</div>
```

In Listing 5-27, we create a parent <div> and assign the **field** class to it. Then we create a child <div> element and assign the **file** container class to it. We assign the primary contextual color to it by using the **is-primary** class in tandem with the **file** class. Next, we define the label using the **file-label** class, the actual interactive and clickable part of the element. Then we define an <input> tag and assign the **file-input** class to it. We define the **type** as **file** and **name** as **resume**. Then we create a parent <span > tag and assign the **file-cta** class to it, which will enable the upload call-to-action. Then, we create a child <span> and define the **file** icon. For this, we assign the **file-icon** class to the child <span> element. The child span element contains the code for the Font Awesome upload icon. Then we create the second <span> child element, to which we assign the **file-label** class and the label as **Click-to-Upload**.

The output of the code so far is shown in Figure 5-27.

Sign Up

Name

Joe Black

Email

✉ jone.black@potterlogic.com   ⚠

Do you mean joe.black@potterlogic.com

✉ Re-enter your Email   ⚠

Password

Enter Password

Re-Enter Password

⬆ Click-to-Upload

Figure 5-27. *Click-to-Upload button added to the form*

Then we create two radio buttons and a checkbox. The code is shown in Listing 5-28.

Listing 5-28. Adding Radio Buttons and Checkbox

```
<div class="control">
  <label class="radio">
    <input type="radio" name="answer">
    Male
  </label>
  <label class="radio">
    <input type="radio" name="answer">
    Female
  </label>
</div>
```

```
<br>
<div class="field">
  <div class="field-body">
    <div class="field">
      <div class="control">
        <label class="checkbox">
          <input type="checkbox">
          <b> Subscribe to our Newsletter</b>
        </label>
      </div>
    </div>
  </div>
</div>
```

In Listing 5-28, we create two radio buttons and a checkbox. Initially, we create a parent <div> element and assign the **control** class to it. Then we create a <label> and assign the **radio** class to it. Then we define the <input> tag, to which we assign the **radio** type attribute. We define the label name as **Male**. Next, we create the second radio button similar to the first one, but here we define the radio button label name as **Female**.

Moving forward, we create a checkbox. We create a parent <div> and assign the field class followed by a child <div> element with the **field-body** class. Then, we create a child <div> element within and assign the **field** class to it. We define a <div> with the control class followed by a label. The **label** class is **checkbox** and the **input type** is **checkbox**. We define the label as **Subscribe to our Newsletter**.

The output of the code is shown in Figure 5-28.

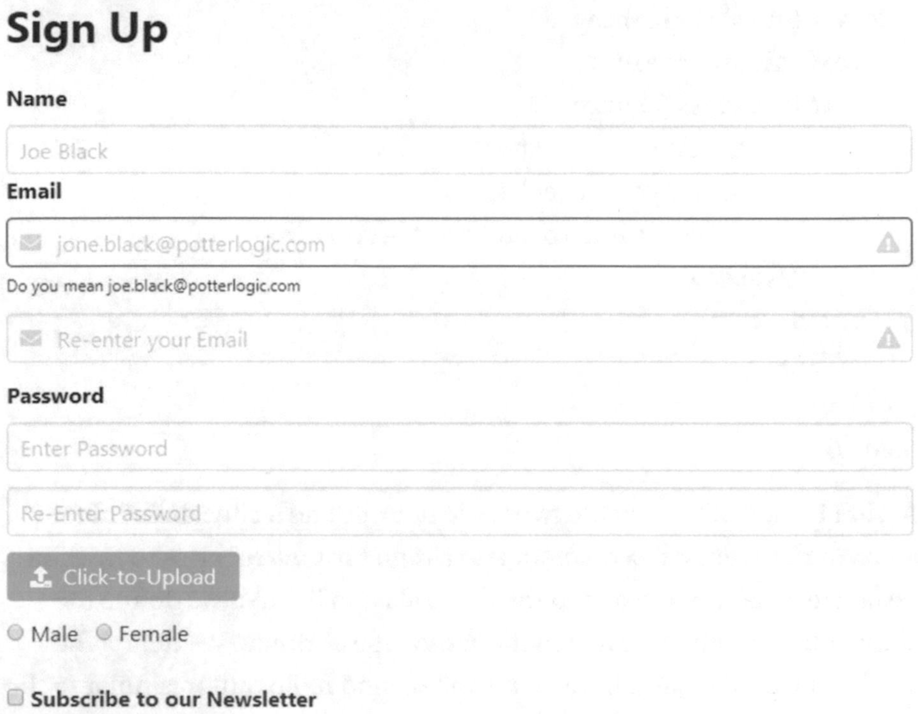

Sign Up

Name

Joe Black

Email

✉ jone.black@potterlogic.com   ⚠

Do you mean joe.black@potterlogic.com

✉ Re-enter your Email   ⚠

Password

Enter Password

Re-Enter Password

⬆ Click-to-Upload

○ Male ○ Female

☐ **Subscribe to our Newsletter**

Figure 5-28. *Adding the radio buttons and the checkbox*

Finally, we create the Submit and Cancel buttons within a <div>, to which we assign the **control** class as shown in Listing 5-29.

Listing 5-29. Adding the Submit and Cancel Buttons

```
<div class="control">
    <button class="button is-success">Submit</button>
    <button class="button is-info">Cancel</button>
</div>
```

The output of the complete code after adding the Submit and Cancel buttons is shown in Figure 5-29.

Sign Up

Name

> Joe Black

Email

> ✉ jone.black@potterlogic.com   ⚠

Do you mean joe.black@potterlogic.com

> ✉ Re-enter your Email   ⚠

Password

> Enter Password

> Re-Enter Password

> ⬆ Click-to-Upload

○ Male   ○ Female

☐ **Subscribe to our Newsletter**

> Submit Cancel

Figure 5-29. *Complete sign up form*

Summary

In this chapter, we learned about Bulma's CSS components that will help build complex web sites with ease. These components adhere to the DRY (Don't Repeat Yourself) paradigm. The common design elements can be reused multiple times, maintaining the concept of clean coding. In the next chapter, we will look at the road ahead for CSS frameworks and the world of possibilities opening up as web design is increasingly leaning toward the digital design paradigm.

CHAPTER 6

Web Design: The Road Ahead

With enterprises undergoing digital transformation, this digital age has been the defining moment for the millennial and Gen Z workforce. Mobile devices have become the de-facto standard for viewing and browsing the Internet. SEO is slowly but surely inclined toward ensuring a user-friendly paradigm.

Simultaneously, web design will undergo a radical shift in the coming years. Personally speaking, web design will evolve at a faster rate along with fast-changing business dynamics. Following are some indications of how it will turn out to be:

- With the advent of digital platforms, web design will transform into digital design, specifically to meet the expectations of the present-day workforce. Ultimately, it is about creating an immersive end-user experience. The gap between the digital world and real-world aspects will be significantly reduced, syncing with each other going forward.

- User experience will be the focal point of web design. Google, Amazon, and Facebook are some organizations that develop advertisements that are much more personalized and user-specific. However, the scope

© Aravind Shenoy 2020
A. Shenoy, *Learning Bulma*, https://doi.org/10.1007/978-1-4842-5482-0_6

is limitless beyond ads, and the future will see digital design showing information that will be more relevant to a particular user or target audience.

- The rapid influx of new gadgets and devices will change web designing trends comprehensively and make virtual reality (VR) and augmented reality (AR) a norm. 3-D effects and high-end virtual effects will be accepted and integrated into digital design, paving the way for more interaction and adoption of real-world facets.

- Today, due to high page load times and latency, 3-D animation, videos, high-resolution images, and automation elements are sparingly used. However, the next-generation web design will focus more on performance, owing to which these high resolution special effects will be displayed quickly just like prose and text content. The dated ways of contemporary web design will be used only for those sites, where text content and detailed description are necessary. After all, it is all about simulating a real-life and immersive experience.

- Gone are the days when you design a site and impose it on users. With data science gaining precedence, data and design cannot be isolated from each other. Data mining and analytics will be a pivotal factor in web design: the data and design experts will collaborate frequently with end-users and the target audience at the center of development. Deciphering user preferences, predictive models, and forecasting trends will play a pivotal role in digital design.

- Voice search is set to be an imperative cog in the wheel of SEO and SEM strategies. Conversational front-end attributes will be incorporated to ensure an interactive and satisfying user experience. In addition, the concerns pertaining to privacy, information safety, and compliance will be addressed with the introduction of a steady and secure structure.

- Machine learning, deep Learning, and artificial intelligence (AI) will be important in the web design arena too. Automated web design is very much possible, mainly due to software-defined patterns. Enterprises will have more control on the design aspects, with less dependence on highly-skilled development staff. Developer tools will empower in-house staff to add custom features and code essential attributes easily, in conjunction with tailored modules for that niche/domain/platform.

- The future of digital web design will be more inclined toward open-source platforms compared to premium, proprietary solutions. Currently, you see established and successful enterprises ruling the roost due to their excellent toolkits and portals. However, this defeats the purpose of the World Wide Web, which was not supposed to be dominated by constraints, monopoly, and technology bias. Industry standards will redefine set patterns to bring more consistency, leaning more toward open-source solutions and protocols—similar to the revolutionary thought processes that led to the Renaissance age and subsequent modernization of humankind in general.

Also, data-driven AI design will transform common enterprise standards and lead to more uniformity across multiple domains.

- Traditionally, JavaScript has been a front-end language, but lately it is being used for server-side programming due to its asynchronous nature and large concurrency capabilities. Reusable components, easy maintenance, and homogenous structures push the case further for total JavaScript adoption. Moreover, systems will get more resilient and the roadblocks associated with security and information safety will be tackled better in the coming years. Therefore, the use of JavaScript will be exponential in the next decade, making it an obvious choice for intuitive web development and design.

The preceding factors are personal predictions and may/may not be realized. In summary, the scope and reach of web design will broaden in conjunction with robotics, AI, and innovation. However, change will be the only constant and maybe the massive technological advances will open up a world of possibilities, akin to the age of the matrix ☺.

Summary

In this book, we learned about the various nuances of the Bulma framework, though we drifted into futuristic prototypes and situations in the end. The last chapter sheds light on the learning curve and situations that will change the way we live and how web design will adapt to those changes.

This book must have definitely helped you get to grips with the awesome Bulma framework. The deeper you delve into the intricacies of Bulma, the greater will be your appreciation for its power and usability. Thank you 👍.

References:

- www.creativebloq.com/features/the-future-of-web-design.

- www.awwwards.com/the-future-of-design-according-to-7-web-visionaries.html.

Index

A

Addons button, 148, 149

B

Breadcrumbs, 90
    code, 90
    conjunction, 94, 95
    container, create, 94
    icons, 97
    separator to arrow
        separator, 91, 92
    sizes, 92
    span tags, 96
    unordered lists, 96
Bulma, 1, 11
    official web page, 3, 4
        desktop site, 4, 5
        mobile, 4
Bulma prototype/starter
        template, 12, 13
Buttons
    addons, 148, 149
    colors, 141
    focus, hover, static, and
        buffering status, 147
    fullwidth, 144, 145
    grouping, 147, 148

    incorporated icons, 156–158
    inverted feature, 145
    list in line, 150
    normal, 141
    outlined, 143, 144
    responsive buttons, 140
    rounded shape, 146
    sizes, 139, 141–143
    types, 140

C

Callout panels, 78
Content wrapper
    CSS modifiers, 158
    ordered lists, 159, 160
    WYSIWYG-generated
        content, 160

D, E

Data mining, 190

F

Flexbox-Powered grid layout
    background color, 16, 17
    column structure, 14–16

A. Shenoy, *Learning Bulma*, https://doi.org/10.1007/978-1-4842-5482-0

L

Layouts
  banners
    color gradient and fullheight
      size, 59
    contextual color, 57, 58
    example, 56, 57
    footer section, 62, 63
    Head and Body code, 60–62
    navigation and footer, 64, 65
  callout panels
    box container, 84
    creating second panel, 81
    creating third panel, 82
    creation, 79
    heading, 79
    mobile phone brands, 80
  cards
    adding content, 68
    adding image, 66, 67
    footer, 69, 71
    is-ancestor class, 72
    mobile screen, 68
  containers and levels
    grid column full width *vs.*
      full HD, 45, 46
    grid column full width *vs.*
      normal, 45
    grid container *vs.* standalone
      element, 43, 44
    levels container
      element, 48, 50
    normal container control *vs.*
      full HD, 47

footers, 85, 87
media object
    image and content, 50, 51
    nested below parent, 53–56
    text area, 52, 53
tiles
    ancestor, creation, 75
    creation, 73
    nested child element, 76, 77
    stacking vertically, 74, 76
    structure, 74

M

Media components
  images
    ratio modifiers, 119–121
    rounded border shape, 119
    same image, different sizes,
      117, 118
  notifications, 115, 117
  pagination
    disabled attribute, 136, 137
    is-rounded class, 135
    module, creation, 130,
      132, 133
    small-, medium-, and
      large-size, 134
  progress bar, 112, 113, 115
  tags
    Addon feature, 125
    append delete button/create
      delete tag, 126, 127
    different Contextual
      Colors, 122